BROADMAN COMMENTS JUL.-SEPT. '96

13 Ready-To-Teach Bible Study Lessons

ROBERT J. DEAN
J. B. FOWLER, JR.
JAMES E. TAULMAN

Based on the International Sunday School Lessons
Each Plan Includes These Sections : ❖ Studying the Bible
❖ Applying the Bible ❖ Teaching the Bible

BROADMAN & HOLMAN PUBLISHERS

Nashville, Tennessee

The Outlines of the International Sunday School Lessons, Uniform Series, are copyrighted by the Committee on the Uniform Series and are used by permission.
Dewey Decimal Classification: 268.61
Printed in the United States of America

Broadman Comments *is published quarterly by Broadman and Holman Publishers, 127 Ninth Avenue, North, Nashville, Tennessee 37234.*
When ordered with other church literature, it sells for $4.99 per quarter.
Second class postage paid at Nashville, Tennessee.

ISSN: 0068-2721
POSTMASTER: Send address change to *Broadman Comments*,
Customer Service Center, 127 Ninth Avenue, North
Nashville, Tennessee 37234

ABBREVIATIONS AND TRANSLATIONS

KJV   *King James Version*

NASB   From the *New American Standard Bible.* © The Lockman Foundation, 1960, 1962, 1963, 1968, 1971, 1972, 1973, 1975, 1977. Used by permission.

NIV   From the Holy Bible, *New International Version.* Copyright © 1973, 1978, 1984 by International Bible Society. Used by permission.

NEB   From *The New English Bible.* Copyright © The Delegates of the Oxford University Press and the Syndics of the Cambridge University Press, 1961, 1970. Reprinted by permission.

NRSV   From the *New Revised Standard Version Bible.* Copyright © 1989, by the Division of Christian Education of the National Council of Churches of Christ in the United States of America, and used by permission.

Contents

God is With Us (Psalms)

God's People Face Judgment

WRITERS

STUDYING THE BIBLE

Robert J. Dean continues the theological traditions of *Broadman Comments* while adding his own fresh insights. Dean is retired from the Baptist Sunday School Board, and is a Th.D. graduate of New Orleans Seminary.

APPLYING THE LESSON

J. B. Fowler, Jr. is a freelance writer from San Antonio, Texas. He has recently retired as editor of *Baptist New Mexican*, Albuquerque, New Mexico.

TEACHING THE CLASS

James E. Taulman is a freelance writer in Nashville, Tennessee. Prior to that, Taulman was an editor of adult Sunday school materials for the Baptist Sunday School Board.

God Is with Us (Psalms)

(July/August)

INTRODUCTION

The Book of Psalms was the hymnbook of the people of Israel. The presence of God is one of the central themes of the psalms. Nearly every psalm is related to the fact that God is present in the world and is lovingly and purposefully involved in the lives of people. The psalms praise God and call for a response to God's presence.

July's lessons entitled, "Praising God," show how the people of God are called to praise: God who creates and sustains (Ps. 104), God who has acted on behalf of His people (Ps. 105), God who delivers from trouble (Ps. 34), and God who knows and cares (Ps. 139).

"Responding to God," is the theme of August's lessons which focus on the following responses: trusting in God (Ps. 40), obeying God's Word (Ps. 119), repenting and confessing (Ps. 51), and worshiping and witnessing (Ps. 96).

God's People Face Judgment

(September)

INTRODUCTION

September's lessons are entitled, "Responses to Wrong," which tell of the reforms of Kings Hezekiah and Josiah. God called Jeremiah as a prophet to proclaim God's word of judgment on the sins of Judah. Habakkuk wrestled with dilemmas of injustice, but committed himself to continue to rejoice in the Lord no matter what happened.

Praising God as Creator and Sustainer

Basic Passage: Psalm 104
Focal Passage: Psalm 104:24–34

P salm 104 is one of the so-called nature psalms. These include Psalms 8; 19; 65; 147; and 148. These psalms deal with the relation of God to His created universe. Psalm 104 is a hymn of praise to God as Creator and Sustainer of the heavens and the earth. The psalm is particularly noted for its descriptions of the interrelations between God and His creation and among the various parts of His creation—animate and inanimate, other forms of life and human life. Thus it may be called the ecology psalm.

▶ ▶ ▶ ▶ **Study Aim:** T*o praise God as Creator and Sustainer of our lives and of all His creations*

STUDYING THE BIBLE

LESSON OUTLINE
  I. Praising God as Creator (Ps. 104:1–9)
    1. A call to praise God (Ps. 104:1)
    2. Creator of the heavens (Ps. 104:2–4)
    3. Creator of earth (Ps. 104:5–9)
  II. Praising God as Sustainer (Ps. 104:10–30)
    1. Sustainer of life (Ps. 104:10–18)
    2. Moon, sun, and time (Ps. 104:19–23)
    3. Praise for the variety and purpose of God's works (Ps. 104:24)
    4. The sea and sea life (Ps. 104:25–26)
    5. Preserver of Life (Ps. 104:27–30)
  III. Praise Ye the Lord (Ps. 104:31–35)
    1. God's enduring glory (Ps. 104:31–32)
    2. Praising the Lord (Ps. 104:33–35)

Psalm 104 begins with a call to bless the Lord and with an actual praise to God (v. 1). In figurative language, the psalmist describes how God created the heavens (vv. 2–4). He created the earth by commanding the water to withdraw, thus making mountains and valleys (vv. 5–9). God sustains life by providing springs and sending rains for man and beast, by providing trees for birds, and by making mountains for mountain animals (vv. 10–18). God gives the sun and moon to provide seasons and to provide night for nocturnal animals and day for man to work (vv.

19–23). The psalmist praised God for the variety and purpose of His works (v. 24). God made and sustains a vast variety of large and small sea life, including the mighty sea monsters, which He made for play (vv. 25–26). God gives food with an open hand to all living things; and although God gives and takes away the breath of life, He continues to renew the earth with new life (vv. 27–30). The psalmist declared the enduring glory of God (vv. 31–32). He committed himself to sing praises to God all his life and to continue to find joy in meditation (vv. 33–35).

I. Praising God as Creator (Ps. 104:1–9)

1. A call to praise God (v. 1). The psalmist called himself to praise the Lord, using the same words with which Psalm 103 begins and ends. Then the psalmist responded to his own call with praise directed to the Lord His God for His greatness, honor, and majesty.

2. Creator of the heavens (vv. 2–4). Using figurative language, the psalmist described God's creation of the heavens. God, who was covered with a garment of light, stretched out the heavens like a man pulling a tent over its frame (v. 2). The clouds became God's chariot and the angels His messengers (vv. 3–4).

3. Creator of earth (vv. 5–9). God laid the foundations of the earth and used water to cover it like a garment (vv. 5–6). At God's thunderous command, the waters receded so that the mountains and valleys were formed (vv. 7–8). God set boundaries for the waters (v. 9).

II. Praising God as Sustainer (Ps. 104:10–30)

1. Sustainer of life (vv. 10–18). God gives springs to provide life-sustaining water for animals and birds (vv. 10–12). From His storehouse, God sends rain to water the earth (v. 13). God makes the grass grow for cattle to eat and provides plants for people to cultivate to produce wine, oil, and bread (vv. 14–15). God, not man, planted the huge cedars of Lebanon (v. 16). God provides trees in which the birds build their nests (v. 17). God made the mountains as home for the wild goats and rock badgers (conies, v. 18).

2. Moon, sun, and time (vv. 19–23). God uses the moon to signal the seasons and tells the sun when to set (v. 19). He provides the night for the nocturnal beasts of the forest (v. 20). The roar of the lions is a prayer to God for food (v. 21). At sunrise the lions go to their dens to rest (v. 22). During the day people arise and go about their work until the evening (v. 23).

3. Praise for the variety and purpose of God's works (v. 24)

24 O Lord, how manifold are thy works! in wisdom hast thou made them all: the earth is full of thy riches.

As the psalmist thought of the variety of God's creative and sustaining works, he was overwhelmed and moved to praise. As the psalmist looked at the vast creations of God and saw God's sustaining work among His creations, he was moved by the unfathomable wisdom of God. He didn't profess to understand all that God had done and was doing, but he was convinced of God's wise and good purpose back of all His workings.

Believers in every age agree with the psalmist. We look at the grandeur of the natural world and at the amazing beings that we humans are. We see the hand of the Creator in both. Although we cannot explain how God created all things or how He goes about sustaining His creation, we see His wisdom and His goodness in ourselves and in the rest of what God created. Like the psalmist, we lift our hearts and voices in praise to God.

4. The sea and sea life (vv. 25–26)

25 So is this great and wide sea, wherein are things creeping innumerable, both small and great beasts.

26 There go the ships: there is that leviathan, whom thou hast made to play therein.

Among God's creations which He sustains is the great and wide sea. The sea teems with living things, both tiny and huge things. The word "creeping" can be translated "teeming" (NIV). Among the huge sea creatures was "leviathan," a giant sea creature that probably was what we call a whale.

Notice what the psalmist says about the purpose of these giant creatures of the sea. God made them to play in the sea. God made them "to frolic there" (NIV). Some scholars think the word means "play with." Nothing is said here about these creatures as food for the benefit of human beings. Instead the Bible says they were created to play in the sea, perhaps even for God Himself to enjoy as they frolicked in the vast sea. Verse 26 doesn't deny that the same creatures were intended for other uses also, but it states their primary purpose as joyful play.

God created human beings as trustees over the rest of creation (Gen. 1:28). Some people have distorted this divine commission as an excuse to plunder and pollute God's creation without respect for all that God created. Only human beings were created in the divine image, but God loves and cares for all His creation. This is one message that is clear in Psalm 104.

5. Preserver of life (vv. 27–30)

27 These wait all upon thee; that thou mayest give them their meat in due season.

28 That thou givest them they gather: thou openest thine hand, they are filled with good.

The "all" refers to all living things, not just to sea life. All living things wait upon their benevolent Creator to provide food at the proper time. The waiting does not mean passive waiting, for living things themselves must gather their food.

However, the bounty they gather are actually good things provided from the open hand of God.

Jesus taught His followers not to be anxious about food and clothing. He told them how the heavenly Father feeds the birds. Then He said that if God so cared for the birds, how much more would He care for His highest creation (see Matt. 6:25–34)?

29 Thou hidest thy face, they are troubled: thou takest away their breath, they die, and return to their dust.

30 Thou sendest forth thy spirit, they are created: and thou re-
newest the face of the earth.

God who created all things sustains all things. He gives the gift of
life, and He brings life to an end. Life is described in verse 29 as
"breath." The Genesis account of the flood refers to living things as having "the breath of life" (see Gen. 6:17; 7:15, 22). Both the Hebrew and
Greek words for "breath" can also be translated "spirit." Thus verse 29
refers to the death that comes to living things when God takes away
their breath, and verse 30 refers to God sending His breath or Spirit to
give the gift of life to living things. Verse 30 affirms the continuing creative work of God as He gives life to succeeding generations of the off-
spring of His original creations. Because people are created in God's
image, we are capable of relating to God in a way that other living things
cannot. However, God is the giver of life and breath to all living things.

III. Praise Ye the Lord (Ps. 104:31–35)

1. God's enduring glory (vv. 31–32)

31 The glory of the Lord shall endure for ever: the Lord shall
rejoice in his works.

As the psalmist looked to the future, he predicted that the glory of the
Lord would last forever. The psalmist pictured God Himself finding joy in
all His works. The verse may be translated as a prayer, "May the glory of
the Lord endure forever" (NIV). If it was a prayer, the prayer was prayed
with confidence that it would be answered. The psalmist was sure that the
eternal Creator and Sustainer's glory would endure forever. He was
prophesying and praying that all beings would join in glorifying God.

32 He looketh on the earth, and it trembleth: he toucheth the
hills, and they smoke.

The psalmist was aware that God the Creator is also God the Judge.
At times He must move with judgment against some of His creatures.
The earth trembles at the look of God when He comes in judgment.
When He touches the hills, they smoke.

2. Praising the Lord (vv. 33–35)

33 I will sing unto the Lord as long as I live: I will sing praise
to my God while I have my being.

This is probably the strongest commitment to praise in Psalm 104,
and one of the strongest in the Bible. First of all, it shows that the
psalmist committed himself to express his praises to God in song. This
makes sense when we remember that the psalms were hymns sung in
Hebrew worship. We also know from experience that singing is a natural as well as a spiritual way to express our praises to God. Paul and Silas
sang praises to God while they were in the Philippian jail (Acts 16:25).
Paul wrote, "Let the word of Christ dwell in you richly in all wisdom;
teaching and admonishing one another in psalms and hymns and spiritual songs, singing with grace in your hearts to the Lord" (Col. 3:16).

The other thing to notice about verse 33 is that the psalmist committed himself to sing praises to the Lord as long as he had life and
breath. This shows that he considered singing praises to God to be an
essential part of life for people of faith.

34 My meditation of him shall be sweet: I will be glad in the Lord.

Singing praises is done openly and often with others. Meditation is more often done silently and alone with God. The psalmist knew that praises to God include both the outward singing of praises and the inner quietness of fellowship with God. Such quiet meditation was sweet to him. It added to the joy and gladness of his life in God.

Verse 35 ends where the psalm began with the psalmist calling himself and others to bless the Lord.

APPLYING THE BIBLE

1. Singing in Sing Sing. B. B. McKinney, a great hymn writer, wrote "Have Faith in God." It is well remembered today. Often he said: "People who can sing and won't sing ought to be sent to Sing Sing and made to sing until they will sing!"

The Book of Psalms was the hymn book of the people of Israel. Singing was a very vital part of their worship experience, and it ought to be a vital part of our worship today. As the psalmist committed himself to be a rejoicing, singing believer all his life, so we should practice the same habit (vv. 33–35).

2. Praise to God. We spend too much time in prayer telling God what we need and too little time praising Him for His goodness and mercy. God wants our praise and rejoices in it. This psalmist knew that well, and opens our lesson today with a strong affirmation of praise to God: "Bless the Lord, O my soul (v. 1), and closes it with the same attitude: "Bless thou the Lord, O my soul. Praise ye the Lord (v. 35).

For a good while, when I was a young pastor, I struggled with the concept of blessing God. How could I possibly bless Him who is everything and has everything? I discovered the answer: by praising His holy name. As God blesses me with manifold blessings, so I can bless Him with manifold praise.

3. The heart of a mouse. There is an old fable about a mouse who was in constant fear of the cat, so a magician turned the mouse into a cat. Then the cat was afraid of the dog, so the magician turned the cat into a dog. Then the dog was afraid of the tiger so the magician turned the dog into a tiger. Immediately, the tiger was afraid of the hunter. Aggravated that he could not satisfy the mouse, the magician said, "Be a mouse again, for you only have the heart of a mouse, and I cannot help you."

The ancient mariners used to pray, "O God, thy sea is so large, and my ship is so small." We have put men on the moon and are now reaching for Mars and outer space. Indeed, how great is God's creation, and how small are we and our ship. But remember that small though we are in a universe with billions upon billions of suns and stars, we are so important that Christ died for us!

4. Animal facts and oddities. Male silkworms have such a keen sense of smell they can detect a female 6 1/2 miles away in the mating season. Flying fish can stay airborne for 1000 feet. Land crabs found in Cuba can run faster than a horse. Tortoises of the Galapagos Islands can live to be 190 years old. Whales weigh 195 tons. Bee humming-birds are so small it takes 18 of them to weigh an ounce. Cobras strike and kill 10,000 people in India alone each year. Gazelles drink no wa-ter. Their chemical processes extract moisture from solid food. Swifts are the world's fastest birds, and can fly up to 200 miles per hour. A human being holds the record for the longest recorded life-span of any known mammal—at least 130 years and perhaps more[1] (according to the Bible many lived much longer). Methuselah lived 969 years (Gen. 5:27), and Noah lived 950 years (Gen. 9:28).

And God not only created them all, but He sustains them (vv. 11–14, 17–18).

5. Facts about the earth. The earth's surface comprises 196,950 square miles, and is the heaviest of all planets, the fifth largest, and the third out from the sun. Its diameter at the equator is 7,926.68 miles, and from pole to pole the diameter is 7,900 miles. Saltwater oceans oc-cupy 72 percent of the earth's surface. Each rotation about its axis re-quires 23 hours, 56 minutes and 4.09 seconds, revolving at a speed of about 17.5 miles per minute. Our earth travels about 18.5 miles per second. The average speed at which our entire solar system is circling within the Milky Way galaxy, of which our earth and solar system are a part, is 180 miles per second. Then why don't we fall off into space in all this movement?[2]

God thought of that, too. One day while Isaac Newton was drinking a cup of tea, he saw an apple fall from a tree. And God told Newton the secret: gravity!

We know far more about the heavens and the earth than did the psalmist. How much more joyously, then, should we shout the benedic-tion, "Praise ye the Lord"?

TEACHING THE BIBLE

▶ *Main Idea:* Praising God as Creator and Sustainer acknowledges our dependence on Him.

▶ *Suggested Teaching Aim:* To lead adults to describe how the psalmist declared his response to God, and to determine how they will praise God.

A TEACHING OUTLINE

1. Use an illustration to introduce the study.
2. Use three listening teams to identify why and how we should praise God.
3. Use brainstorming to list ways members can praise God in their lives.

Introduce the Bible Study

Read "Facts about the earth" from "Applying the Bible" to intro-duce the lesson. Point out that the Creator of this marvelous earth is worthy of all praise.

Search for Biblical Truth

IN ADVANCE, make a unit poster and include the title of the lesson, the psalms being studied, and the date. Display this each week. Use an arrow cut from brightly colored paper to indicate which lesson is being studied each week.

Enlist two other people to help you introduce the unit. Give one person a copy of the paragraph describing Unit I and give the other person a copy of the paragraph describing Unit II ("Introduction"). Read the first paragraph yourself and then call for the other two readers to read theirs. Point out that for the next two months you will be studying various psalms.

Point out today's lesson on the unit poster. Use "Studying the Bible" to briefly summarize Psalm 104:10–23. Ask a volunteer to read 104:24–32. On a chalkboard or a large sheet of paper, write: Why we should praise the Lord? As the reader reads ask members to listen for reasons the psalmist and we should praise God. Ask a third of the class to be responsible for 104:24–26; a third to be responsible for 104:27–30; and a third to be responsible for 104:31–32.

Ask the first group to share reasons the psalmist gave for praising God. (Their answers may differ but consider: *works, wisdom, riches, sea.*) Write their responses on the chalkboard or large sheet of paper.

Ask the second group to share reasons the psalmist gave for praising God. (Provides food for creation, controls life and death, creates by His Spirit.)

Be prepared to share information from "Studying the Bible" that would help members understand these reasons.

Ask the third group to share reasons the psalmist gave for praising God. (Glory of the Lord, judgment.)

Write on the chalkboard or large sheet of paper: How should we praise the Lord? Ask a volunteer to read 104:33–34. Ask members to list ways the psalmist suggested he would praise the Lord. (Sing as long as he had breath, meditate, be glad.)

Give the Truth a Personal Focus

Ask members to suggest ways this psalm would help them to praise the Lord in a contemporary setting. List all of the ideas on the chalkboard or large sheet of paper. Encourage members to list all ideas that come to their minds. After all the ideas have been listed, go back over the list and ask members silently to choose the two that would appeal most to them. Then ask members to choose one of these two that they will apply to their lives this week. Allow about two or three minutes for members to list some ways they will put this method of praise in practice.

Close by asking members to turn to 104:35 and read the last part of the verse in unison. Even if they have various translations, ask them to read aloud.

---

1. Adapted from David Wallenchinsky and Irving Wallace, *The People's Almanac* (Garden City, N.Y.: Doubleday and Co., 1975), 695.

2. Ibid., 678.

Praising God for Mighty Acts

Basic Passage: Psalm 105
Focal Passages: Psalms 105:1-11, 43–45

P salm 105 is one of the hymns that reminded the Hebrews of
God's acts in history (see also Pss. 78; 106; and 114). The psalm
recited God's past acts of deliverance and guidance in the life of
Israel. The remembrance of God's mighty acts moved the people to
praise God and bear testimony to Him. The first part of Psalm 105 (vv.
1–15) was sung along with Psalm 96 and part of Psalm 106 when the
ark of the covenant was brought to Jerusalem (see 1 Chron. 16; see
vv. 8–22).

▶ ▶ ▶ ▶ ▶ ▶ ▶ ▶ ▶ **Study Aim:** *To praise God for His mighty acts of deliverance*
for His people

STUDYING THE BIBLE

LESSON OUTLINE
I. Call to Remember, Testify, and Worship (Ps. 105:1–6)
  1. Give thanks, pray, sing praises, and testify (Ps. 105:1–2)
  2. Glory in His name and seek His presence (Ps. 105:3–4)
  3. Remember His mighty acts (Ps. 105:5–6)
II. Remembering the God Who Remembers (Ps. 105:7–45)
  1. Sovereign Lord over all (Ps. 105:7)
  2. The God who remembers His covenant (Ps. 105:8–11)
  3. Leading and protecting the patriarchs (Ps. 105:12–15)
  4. Bringing good out of evil in the life of Joseph
     (Ps. 105:16–23)
  5. Delivering Israel from Egypt (Ps. 105:24–38)
  6. Guided and fed in the wilderness (Ps. 105:39–41)
  7. Praise the God who remembers His covenant
     (Ps. 105:42–45)

The psalmist called people to give thanks, pray, sing, and testify (vv.
1–2). He called them to glory in God and seek His presence (vv. 3–4).
Above all, they were to remember God and His mighty works on their
behalf (vv. 5–6). They confessed their faith in the sovereign Lord of all
the earth (v. 7). God remembered His covenant with Abraham, Isaac,
and Jacob—to bring their descendants into the land of Canaan (vv.
8–11). God guided and protected the patriarchs (vv. 12-15). He
brought good out of evil and used Joseph to provide care for his family
(vv. 16–23). When the Israelites were mistreated in Egypt, God's
mighty power delivered them and blessed them (vv. 24–38). The Lord
led Israel and fed them in the wilderness (vv. 39–41). Since God faith-

fully remembered His promise to give Israel the land, they should obey His laws and praise Him (vv. 42–45).

I. Call to Remember, Testify, and Worship (Ps. 105:1-6)

1. Give thanks, pray, sing praises, and testify (vv. 1–2)

1 O give thanks unto the Lord; call upon His name: make known his deeds among the people.

2 Sing unto him, sing psalms unto him: talk ye of all his wondrous works.

Verses 1–2 provide a call to worship. The people of Israel were called to do four things: (1) give thanks to the Lord for His deliverance and blessings, (2) call on His name in confession and prayer, (3) sing praises to the Lord, and (4) declare and show God's mighty acts among the people of the world. These four aspects of worship form the structure of worship in every generation. When we come together to worship God, we give thanks to God for His blessings, we lift our hearts to Him in prayer, we sing praises to Him, and we proclaim His mighty acts to all.

2. Glory in His name and seek His presence (vv. 3–4)

3 Glory ye in his holy name: let the heart of them rejoice that seek the Lord.

4 Seek the Lord, and his strength: seek his face evermore.

The call to worship continued in verses 3–4. Verse 3 affirms a fact about true worship. Those who worship the Lord glory in Him and His holy character. True worship is a joyful experience of celebration of God's past blessings and abiding presence with His people. Verse 4 is a call for people of faith to seek the Lord in this kind of true worship. These words were used to summon people to join other worshipers on the way to God's sanctuary. They were to join others in seeking God's presence and in drawing fresh strength from His presence.

Even in biblical times, some would-be worshipers were neglecting the assembling of themselves together (see Heb. 10:25). God's Word summons all people of faith not to neglect this essential aspect of life. Our faith needs to be expressed and our spiritual life needs to be renewed in worship.

3. Remember His mighty acts (vv. 5–6)

5 Remember his marvellous works that he hath done; his wonders, and the judgments of his mouth;

6 O ye seed of Abraham his servant, ye children of Jacob his chosen.

The word *remember* is an important word in the Old Testament, the key to Psalm 105, and an essential element in true faith. In the Old Testament, "remember" was used repeatedly to call the people of Israel to remember God and what He had done for His people. Deuteronomy especially emphasizes the need to remember. At the end of the Fourth Commandment are these words, "And remember that thou wast a servant in the land of Egypt, and that the Lord thy God brought thee out thence through a mighty hand and by a stretched out arm" (Deut. 5:15). As the Israelites prepared to enter Canaan, Moses warned them not to forget, but to "remember the Lord thy God" (Deut. 8:18).

Psalm 105:1–6 forms a call to worship by remembering the mighty acts of the Lord. The body of the psalm is a summary of some of these mighty acts of the Lord. Beginning with God's covenant with Abraham, Isaac, and Jacob, the psalmist recited God's acts of deliverance for His people until He led them into the promised land.

People of faith in every generation must know who they are and whose they are. An essential to achieving this is remembering the mighty acts of God in the past—not just our individual pasts, but His past dealings with His people. Some people claim to hate history. Others do their best to ignore history. The Bible, in its divine wisdom, calls us to remember history, because eyes of faith see history as "His story."

People of faith see the hand of God in the events of history. The Bible was written by people of such faith who under the Spirit's direction highlighted the mighty acts of God on our behalf. Psalm 105 ends with the entry into Canaan, but the rest of the Old Testament adds to His story; and the New Testament tells of the coming, life, death, and resurrection of God's Son, Jesus Christ. When we worship, we begin by remembering, thanking God, and proclaiming what God has done, is doing, and will do.

II. Remembering the God Who Remembers (Ps. 105:7–45)

1. Sovereign Lord over all (v. 7)

7 He is the Lord our God: his judgments are in all the earth.

The main section of the psalm begins with a confession of faith. The word translated "Lord" is "Yahweh," the personal name of God as He had revealed Himself to His chosen people. He was their God in a special way, but the psalmist recognized that He was also sovereign Lord over all the earth.

2. The God who remembers His covenant (vv. 8–11)

8 He hath remembered his covenant for ever, the word which he commanded to a thousand generations.

The same word for *remember* is used in verse 5 of Israel's need to remember the Lord and in verse 8 of the Lord's remembering of His covenant with the people of Israel. In other words, Psalm 105 is a call to remember the God who remembers. In both cases, *remember* means more than "having a memory of something." The word includes the meaning of "being faithful to what has been promised." As applied to the Lord, it meant that He would faithfully fulfill His promises to Israel. As applied to Israel, it called on them to remember what God had done for them and remain faithful to Him.

9 Which covenant he made with Abraham, and his oath unto Isaac;

10 And confirmed the same unto Jacob for a law, and to Israel for an everlasting covenant:

11 Saying, Unto thee will I give the land of Canaan, the lot of your inheritance.

Verses 9–11 focus on the covenant God made. He made it with Abraham (see Gen. 15:18–21). God renewed it with Isaac (see Gen. 26:2–5). The Lord repeated the covenant promise to Jacob (see Gen. 28:13–15). Jacob's name was changed to Israel, and His descendants became the children of Israel. The covenant with Abraham, Isaac, and Jacob thus was a covenant with all Israel. The covenant with Israel was sealed at Mount Sinai (see Ex. 19:1–6). A central feature of the covenant was to give the children of Israel the land of Canaan. The rest of Psalm 105 reminded later generations of Israelites how God faithfully kept that promise.

3. Leading and protecting the patriarchs (vv. 12–15). Having mentioned the patriarchs in verses 9–10, the psalmist described how they were few in number and sojourners in the lands through which they journeyed (vv. 12–13). God preserved and protected them from their powerful enemies (vv. 14–15).

4. Bringing good out of evil in the life of Joseph (vv. 16–23). God used a famine as an indirect blessing (v. 16). He allowed Joseph to pass through severe trials (vv. 17–19) before elevating him and using him to deliver his people (vv. 20–22). As a result, Jacob and all his family moved to Egypt, thus setting the stage for the next act of divine deliverance (v. 23).

5. Delivering Israel from Egypt (vv. 24–38). When the Israelites prospered, the Egyptians grew to hate them (vv. 24–25). God sent Moses and Aaron (v. 26), but the real deliverer was God Himself who sent the plagues on Egypt (vv. 27–36). The enslaved Israelites left Egypt with the wealth of Egypt, and the Egyptians were glad to see them go because of the mighty power of God (vv. 37–38).

6. Guided and fed in the wilderness (vv. 39–41). God led His people by the cloud and pillar of fire (v. 39). He fed them with manna and quail, and gave them water from a rock (vv. 40–41).

7. Praise the God who remembers His covenant (vv. 42–45). The final verses of the chapter tie back in to verses 8–11. God did indeed remember His covenant (v. 42).

> **43 And he brought forth His people with joy, and his chosen with gladness:**
>
> **44 And gave them the lands of the heathen: and they inherited the labour of the people.**

When God brought His chosen people out of Egypt, they celebrated His deliverance with songs of joy (see Exod. 15:1–22). When the Lord brought the people of Israel into the promised land, He pointed out to them that the land was a gift from Him. They received cities and houses they had not built, wells they had not dug, and crops they had not planted (Deut. 6:9–11).

> **45 That they might observe his statutes, and keep his laws. Praise ye the Lord.**

Verse 45 sums up the twofold response that the people should make as they remembered the God who remembered His covenant with them. First, they should fulfill their covenant responsibilities by keeping the statutes and laws that the Lord gave them. Second, they should continually praise the Lord. This twofold response reminds us that no worship is acceptable to God unless it includes a life that is lived for the Lord. It also should remind us that living for such a God ought not to be a burden. People of faith in the Old Testament spoke of God's law as sweet and joyful (see Ps. 19:7–14).

They didn't separate daily living and times of worship into two compartments. Instead they saw all of life as times of joyful praise to God and testimony to others. In a passage in which Peter addressed Christians as God's New Testament chosen people, he wrote "that ye should shew forth the praises of him who hath called you out of darkness into his marvellous light" (1 Pet. 2:9).

APPLYING THE BIBLE

1. Every day is Thanksgiving Day. In America, we celebrate Thanksgiving Day every November. But for each of us every day ought to be thanksgiving day. Let us begin each day with a prayer of thanksgiving to God, and close each day with a benediction of thanksgiving. This is what the psalmist did. Every day was a day of thanksgiving for this ancient writer.

For what do we have to be thankful? Each of us will have to make an answer. Among these blessings are America, where we are free; our church, where we can worship without fear; our home which shelters us; an abundance of food while millions are starving; medical care which is the best in the world; and loved ones and friends who befriend and encourage us. The list is endless. Above all, we ought to rejoice in our Savior, who forgives our sins and promises a home in heaven for every believer.

The psalmist encourages us to make abundant thanksgiving a daily part of our lives: "O give thanks unto the Lord." How often does the refrain echo in the Psalms?

2. "The Lord He walks here." The late R. L. Middleton once told about a woman who was in Charleston, S. C., with her husband as he waited to sail overseas. It was wartime. Things were so uncertain, and the woman's heart was terribly burdened. She and her husband and three-year-old son walked in the Magnolia Gardens, and although there were hundreds of people walking through the gardens, it was as quiet and reverent as a cathedral.

Coming upon a black gardener down on his knees tending the flowers, the lady thanked him for his careful work in caring for the gardens and then commented on how quiet and reverent the garden was.

Rising slowly from his knees, and with a faraway look in his eyes, the old man put his gnarled hand on the little boy's golden curls and replied: "Yes, ma'am, there is a reason. You see, the Lord—He walks here, too."

The psalmist was recalling in our study today the presence of God with the struggling, wandering patriarchs and with the Israelites from the time of their father Abraham until they settled in Canaan (vv. 5–45). He was reminding them of the spiritual blessings and how Almighty God had walked with them all the way.

Look back over your life. In your greatest joys and severest hardships can you not also say, "He has walked with me all the way"?

3. Walking by faith. The Bible tells us that we walk by faith and not by sight. It also warns us that without faith we cannot please God. But what is faith? One definition of faith that is adequate for me declares that faith is whole-soul trust in God. I use my intelligence, my instincts, my experience in making decisions, but place it all under the faith God has given me. Faith calls the final shot. Faith is not leaping out into the darkness; rather it is walking in the light.

God is the giver of faith. It is not some emotion we work up in ourselves. But faith comes as we pour daily over God's Word and act on what it teaches us (Rom. 10:17, NIV).

As though he were speaking for all the nation and its past history, the psalmist confesses his faith in God. The word *Lord* is the personal name as he revealed Himself to His people. Faith is a personal relationship with God.

4. No mountain too steep for two. Henrik Ibsen (1828–1906) was a noted Norwegian writer and dramatist who is considered the father of modern drama. In one of his books, he describes two people attempting a very dangerous mountain climb in Norway. Friends tried to dissuade them, warning them of the dangers, but the climbers were determined to go. To those trying to discourage them, one of the climbers shouted, "There is no precipice too steep for two."

The psalmist notes this. In Israel's founding as a nation (vv. 5–12), in her slavery in Egypt (vv. 23–36), in her deliverance from Egypt (vv. 37–43), and in her settling in Canaan (vv. 44–45), God was with her all the way. The psalmist now calls on Israel to remember (v. 5) that she was never alone. God was with her all the way. It's worth remembering that none of us walks alone. God walks by our side until the going is too hard for us to bear. Then, as if we were a wounded sheep, He carries us in his arms.

TEACHING THE BIBLE

▶ *Main Idea:* Believers should always praise God for His mighty acts.
▶ *Suggested Teaching Aim:* To lead adults to describe how the psalmist praised God for His mighty acts of deliverance, and to praise God for the way God has delivered them.

A TEACHING OUTLINE

1. Introduce the Bible study with an illustration.
2. Use a responsive reading to present the biblical text.
3. Use Scripture examination and group discussion to study the Bible.
4. Use listmaking to help members apply the Scripture to their lives.

Introduce the Bible Study

Use "Every day is Thanksgiving Day" from "Applying the Bible" to begin the session. Read the "Main Idea" and ask members as they study the lesson to be thinking about ways they can praise God for delivering them.

Search for Biblical Truth

IN ADVANCE, enlist two readers to prepare a responsive reading of the Scripture text. The psalms are poetry. Generally, the first line or part of a line will make a statement and the second line or part of a line will make a parallel statement. Have one person read the first statement and the second to read the second. Call for them to read the whole Scripture at this time.

Ask members to open their Bibles to 105:1–2. Ask: What four actions did the psalmist call for Israel to take? (Give thanks, call, sing, declare/talk.)
DISCUSS: How are these four actions still evident in our current worship services?

Ask members to look at 105:3–4. Ask: What should be the attitude of worshipers based on these two verses? (Glory, rejoice, seek God)
DISCUSS: How does seeking the Lord encourage us to worship God regularly? How does regular worship help us in our daily lives?

Ask members to look at 105:5–6. Using the information in "Studying the Bible," lecture briefly on the importance of the word *remember.* Write this definition of *remember* from "Studying the Bible": "Being faithful to what has been promised." In your lecture point out: (1) how the word *remember* is used in the Old Testament; (2) the psalmist calls for Israel to remember God's mighty acts; (3) people of faith need to remember all of God's mighty acts throughout history; (4) the Bible is a record of the remembrance of many people over a long period of time.
DISCUSS: What role has remembering played in your Christian life?

Ask members to look at 105:7–8. Using the information in "Studying the Bible," explain how Psalm 105 is a call to remember the God who remembers.
DISCUSS: Refer to the definition of *remember* and ask: Does the definition support God's remembering more than human remembering?

Ask members to look at 9–11. Ask: What did the covenant with Abraham, Isaac, and Jacob involve? (Covenant with all Israel that God would be their God and give them Canaan.)
DISCUSS: Which features of this covenant were conditional and which were unconditional?

Ask members to look at 105:43–45. Ask: What was the attitude of the people when they left Egypt? (Joy.) What response did God expect the people to make to Him? (Observe statues/keep laws and praise Him.)

Give the Truth a Personal Focus

Read 105:5. Ask members to remember ways God has delivered them. List these on a chalkboard or large sheet of paper. When all have listed the ways God has delivered them, read 105:45. Point out that God's graciousness in delivering us involves our keeping God's laws and praising Him. Share "The doxology" from "Applying the Bible" for next week (July 21). Close by singing or reading the "doxology."

Praising God for Deliverance

Basic Passage: Psalm 34
Focal Passages: Psalm 34:2–10,18–22

P salm 34 is one of many psalms that praise God for delivering His
people. The writer of Psalm 34 bore testimony to God's goodness and deliverance in times of trouble. The superscription to
Psalm 34 attributes the psalm to David, citing one of the many occasions when the Lord delivered David from danger (see 1 Sam.
21:10–15). The psalmist called others to worship using a personal testimony of divine deliverance from troubles (vv. 1–10). He instructed others in the good life and on trusting God in times of trouble (vv. 11–22).

▶ ▶ ▶ ▶ **Study Aim:** *To bear testimony to God's help in times of*
trouble

STUDYING THE BIBLE

LESSON OUTLINE
I. **Worship, Testimony, and Invitation (Ps. 34:1–10)**
1. Call to magnify God (Ps. 34:1–3)
2. Testimony of deliverance (Ps. 34:4–7)
3. Invitation to experience God's goodness (Ps. 34:8–10)
II. **Instructions and Affirmations of Trust (Ps. 34:11–22)**
1. Instructions for the good life (Ps. 34:11–14)
2. Two views of God (Ps. 34:15–17)
3. Trust during times of trouble (Ps. 34:18–22)

The psalmist committed himself to praise God and called others to
join in magnifying the Lord (vv. 1–3). He testified how God had delivered him and affirmed that the Lord is with His people to deliver them
(vv. 4–7). He called others to taste and see that the Lord is good (vv.
8–10). The young were instructed that the good life consists of turning
from evil, doing good, and seeking peace (vv. 11–14). The Lord's face
is turned toward the righteous to help them, but against the wicked to
cut them off (vv. 15–17). The righteous are not immune from trouble
but have the assurance of the Lord's deliverance (vv. 18–22).

I. Worship, Testimony, and Invitation (Ps. 34:1–10)

1. **Call to magnify God (vv. 1–3).** The psalmist declared that he
would bless the Lord at all times, not just when his heart was filled with
gratitude for a special deliverance (v. 1).

**2 My soul shall make her boast in the Lord: the humble shall
hear thereof, and be glad.**

3 O magnify the Lord with me, and let us exalt his name to-gether.

The Bible often uses the word "boast" to describe selfish, sinful boasting. People boast of their riches (Ps. 49:6), of their sins (Ps. 52:1), of their idols (Ps. 97:7), and of their plans for the future (Prov. 27:1). Psalm 34:2 boldly uses this same word to describe boasting, not of oneself, but in the Lord. The same Hebrew word is sometimes translated "glory in."

When a person of faith boasts in the Lord, other people of humble faith have their hearts warmed by such testimonies. Thus the writer of Psalm 34 called others to join him in magnifying the Lord and in exalting Him together. The psalm thus stresses sharing personal testimonies with one another as an encouragement for all to join in praising the name of the Lord.

2. Testimony of deliverance (vv. 4–7)

4 I sought the Lord, and he heard me, and delivered me from all my fears.

The word for seeking the Lord often was used of seeking the Lord in worship at His sanctuary (Ps. 24:6). Thus the psalmist may have been telling of a prayer for deliverance made at the place of worship. Of course, people of faith know that such prayers can be prayed wherever we are. At any rate, the Lord heard the prayer and delivered the psalmist from all his fears. The word "fears" may refer to the things that he feared, or it may refer to his fear of those things. Sometimes the Lord removes the causes of our fears; when He doesn't, He still provides courage to face our fears (see 2 Tim. 1:7).

5 They looked unto him, and were lightened: and their faces were not ashamed

Verse 5 moved from the psalmist's personal experience to the experience of all those who seek the Lord. "Lightened" means "are radiant." Their lives shined, and they were not ashamed because they received the help they needed.

6 This poor man cried, and the Lord heard him, and saved him out of all his troubles.

Verse 6 is expressed in the third person, but the psalmist was probably using this mode of expression to continue his personal testimony of deliverance. In other words, the "poor man" may have been the writer himself. In any case, the testimony is one that any person of faith can give when the Lord delivers the person from troubles or, more often, delivers him through troubles.

7 The angel of the Lord encampeth round about them that fear him, and delivereth them.

The angel of the Lord is the messenger of God, sometimes a personal manifestation of the Lord (see Judg. 6:11–23). At times, the angel of the Lord revealed Himself in visible form to people of faith. The psalmist was affirming that even when the angel of the Lord was not seen with the physical eyes, people of faith could be aware of His gracious, protecting presence. One such occasion is described in 2 Kings 6:14–17. A Syrian army had surrounded the city of Samaria. Elisha's servant was filled with fear and asked: "'What shall we do?' 'Don't be afraid,' the prophet answered. 'Those who are with us are more than those who are with them.' And Elisha prayed, 'O Lord, open his eyes so he may see.' Then the Lord opened the servant's eyes, and he looked and saw the hills full of horses and chariots of fire all around Elisha" (2 Kings 6:15–17, NIV).

3. Invitation to experience God's goodness (vv. 8–10)

8 O taste and see that the Lord is good: blessed is the man that trusteth in him.

The experience of the psalmist had reinforced his trust in the goodness of God. This is a basic tenet of biblical faith. The child prays, "God is great; God is good." All theology is summed up in this simple affirmation. Some people are overwhelmed at the greatness of God, but lack trust in the goodness of God, whom we call our heavenly Father. We stand in reverence before His greatness; we trust His goodness.

As the psalmist testified to God's goodness, he invited others to experience the goodness of God for themselves. Like someone who had tried a new kind of food and found it delicious, he invited others to taste and see that the Lord is good. Nothing can take the place of personal experience. People can hear from others that God is good, but until they trust Him for themselves, their belief falls short of true faith. When Philip was telling his friend Nathanael about Jesus of Nazareth, Nathanael asked, "Can there any good thing come out of Nazareth?" Philip wisely answered, "Come and see" (John 1:46).

9 O fear the Lord, ye his saints: for there is no want to them that fear him.

No contradiction exists between the calls to trust God and to fear Him. Because of His greatness and holiness, we bow in His presence with reverence and awe.

10 The young lions do lack, and suffer hunger: but they that seek the Lord shall not want any good thing.

Lions have always represented strength; for example, people call the lion the king of the jungle. The psalmist used young lions as symbols of physical strength. Such strength fails to achieve its goals. By contrast, those who seek the Lord find in Him all they want and need. The great and good God does not withhold from His own what they need to do His will (see Matt. 6:33; 7:7–11; Phil. 4:13).

II. Instructions and Affirmations of Trust (Ps. 34:11–22)

1. Instructions for the good life (vv. 11–14).

The psalmist moved from testimony to teaching. Based on his experience, he began to teach young people to fear and trust God (v. 11). He asked if they did not want to live the good life (v. 12). Then he instructed them in how to live the good life: by avoiding sins of the tongue (v. 13), by turning from evil and doing good, and by seeking peace (v. 14).

2. Two views of God (vv. 15–17).

God's eyes are upon the righteous, and His ears are open to their prayers (v. 15). By contrast, God's face is set against those who persist in their evil (v. 16). Earlier the psalmist had testified of his own experience of divine deliverance (vv. 4, 6) and had affirmed that God delivers His people when they seek Him (vv. 5, 7). In verse 17, he repeated that affirmation.

3. Trust during times of trouble (vv. 18–22)

18 The Lord is nigh unto them that are of a broken heart; and saveth such as be of a contrite spirit.

The word "contrite" may be translated "crushed" (NIV). Thus the psalmist may have been affirming that the Lord helps those whose hearts have been broken and whose spirits have been crushed by troubles. If "contrite" is the correct meaning, his point was that those who pray to God must come with broken hearts and contrite spirits because of their sins. Deciding between these two meanings is hard, because both are clearly taught elsewhere in the Bible. God's concern for the poor and brokenhearted is clear (see Isa. 61:1; Luke 4:18; Matt. 11:28). At the same time, true repentance involves what David called "a broken spirit: a broken and a contrite heart" (Ps. 51:17).

19 Many are the afflictions of the righteous: but the Lord delivereth him out of them all.

Psalm 34 does not teach that the righteous are exempt from troubles; indeed verse 19 acknowledges that they suffer many afflictions. The last part of verse 19 could be taken to mean that the Lord always delivers His people from every evil situation. The personal experiences of people of faith show that sometimes God delivers His people from the hands of evil and evildoers. The experiences of the three Hebrew children and of Daniel are memorable examples of such deliverances (see Dan. 3; 6). The experiences of John the Baptist, Paul, and Jesus Himself show that sometimes God allows people of faith to suffer and to die. However, God always is with His people to deliver them through troubles and from the ultimate power of death itself.

20 He keepeth all his bones: not one of them is broken.

Broken bones in the Old Testament stand for broken health (see Ps. 51:8; Isa. 38:13) or for oppression (see Mic. 3:3). Thus not to have bones broken signified health and security.

21 Evil shall slay the wicked: and they that hate the righteous shall be desolate.

God created a moral and spiritual universe. Those who do evil break the laws of this universe and bring judgment on themselves. Moses said, "Be sure your sin will find you out" (Num. 32:23). Paul warned, "Be not deceived; God is not mocked: for whatsoever a man soweth, that shall he also reap" (Gal. 6:7). In the same way, Psalm 34:21 says that "evil shall slay the wicked." God stands back of such judgment, but the responsibility for spiritual desolation belongs to those who choose the way of evil.

22 The Lord redeemeth the soul of his servants: and none of them that trust in him shall be desolate.

Sinners are to blame for their own desolation; but the righteous cannot take credit for escaping desolation. Rather, they have been redeemed by the Lord. The word *redeem* is a familiar biblical idea. Slaves were redeemed from their plight. The Israelites were redeemed from Egypt. Sinners are redeemed from sin and death through the death of God's Son for us (see Rom. 3:24; Eph. 1:7). The response of God's people to such goodness is to trust their Redeemer.

APPLYING THE BIBLE

1. The doxology. In many churches across the land this morning, the doxology will be sung by thousands of worshipers. It is a hymn of praise to the Holy Trinity: "Praise God from whom all blessing flow; . . . Praise Father, Son, and Holy Ghost."

One night during the Civil War, new Confederate prisoners were being brought into Libby Prison. Among them was a young Baptist minister who almost fainted when he saw the sick, dying, and the filth and squalor. Heartbroken over what he saw, he sat down, put his face in his hands and began to weep. Just then, a lone voice began to sing among the prisoners, "Praise God from whom all blessing flow." Soon, nearly all the prisoners were singing. As the song died away, the young minister stood and sang alone: "Prisons would palaces prove/If Jesus would dwell with me there."

The doxology was written by Rev. Thomas Ken, whom King Charles II made a chaplain to his sister, Mary, Princess of Orange. Ken was so courageous in his preaching that the king often said on his way to chapel, "I must go and hear Ken tell me my faults."

Burdens are lifted, light shines on our pathway, and comfort comes when we focus, not on our problems and trials, but on the goodness of God (vv. 1–3). Practice singing the great hymns of faith, both in public and in private, when your spirits are low. It's good therapy.

2. God's providential care. Each of us, no doubt, can testify to how God has delivered us from some sore trial or from danger. Perhaps He has lifted you out of a deep depression, healed you when all hope was gone, or spared you from a tragic death. Think back, and you will remember some time in your life when the angels of God which, perhaps, you have never considered, delivered you from death (v. 7).

In my last pastorate, a godly mother told me about being awakened deep in the night concerned about her son who was on the highway. She knew something was wrong and began to pray for his safety. Later, he came home and told her about being in an automobile accident that nearly took his life. Another godly saint, who was all but bedfast, related to me that in the quiet of the night she would hear her wooden floors creak. "I knew," she said, "that the angels were surrounding me and watching over me" (Heb. 1:13–14).

This psalm, which is attributed to David, testifies to God's watchcare over and presence with His people at all times, but especially in times of grave crises (vv. 4–7).

3. God is good. Many of us taught our children their first prayer: "God is great/God is good/Let us thank Him for our food." Indeed, God is good as the psalmist stated in vv. 8-10. He then points out that although members of the animal kingdom may suffer from "lack and hunger," God will lavish His love and care upon those who "seek the Lord." They shall "not want any good thing."

Consider the goodness of God poured out upon you: you are well enough to be in church today; you will enjoy a good meal after church in a starving world; you will be sheltered from the July heat in an adequate, air-conditioned home; you will rest safely tonight in your bed—on and on we could go.

With God's goodness so abundantly lavished on us, how foolish we are to complain about things that really matter very little.

4. The need for America to have a "great awakening." There was a period in America's colonial history known as "The Great Awakening" (1740–1745). One of the prime movers of the Great Awakening, which swept through the colonies bringing thousands to Jesus, was Jonathan Edwards, the Congregationalist minister in Northhampton, Massachusetts. His sermon preached there in 1741, "Sinners in the Hands of an Angry God," was used mightily of God to ignite the Great Awakening.

It is recorded that as Edwards preached that now famous sermon, the Holy Spirit swept over the congregation and people held on to the backs of their pews, with white knuckles, crying out to God to save them.

Oh, how America needs that kind of preaching and that kind of awakening. We have lost our fear of God and crime runs rampant across the land!

Billy Graham says that if God does not judge America for her wickedness, then He must apologize to Sodom and Gomorrah! Amen!

TEACHING THE BIBLE

▶ *Main Idea:* Believers who have been delivered will want to praise God.

▶ *Suggested Teaching Aim:* To lead adults to describe how the psalmist said God had delivered him, and to write their own testimony of deliverance.

A TEACHING OUTLINE

1. Use an illustration to begin the session.

2. Use group activity—including paraphrasing and group discussion—to study the Bible.

3. Use a written testimony to help members express their gratitude for God's deliverance in times of trouble.

Introduce the Bible Study

Use "God's providential care" in "Applying the Bible" to introduce the session.

Search for Biblical Truth

IN ADVANCE, print two strip posters with the major points of the lesson: "I. Worship, Testimony, and Invitation (Ps. 34:1–10)" and "II.

Instructions and Affirmations of Trust (Ps. 34:11–22)." Place the first poster on the focal wall at this point.

IN ADVANCE, write the following instructions on a chalkboard or a large sheet of paper (or write them on five small slips of paper to give out individually):

1. Read your assigned Scripture in as many different translations as you can.
2. Read any quarterlies or commentaries you have available.
3. Discuss the verse.
4. Paraphrase the verse.
5. Develop one discussion question to use with the whole class.

To model what you want members to do, ask members to turn to 34:2–3. Ask for as many different translations to be read of the verses as possible. (You may want to bring translations you know your members will not have.) Use the information in "Studying the Bible" to explain what the verses mean. Point out that the psalm stresses sharing personal testimonies with one another as an encouragement for all to join in praising the name of the Lord. Tell them to be thinking of how they can write a personal testimony at the conclusion of the lesson.

Ask members to paraphrase these two verses.

DISCUSS: How can a person "boast" in the Lord? What benefit is it?

Organize the class in five groups and make the following assignments:

Group 1—Psalm 34:4–5
Group 2—Psalm 34:6–7
Group 3—Psalm 34:8–10
Group 4—Psalm 34:18–20
Group 5—Psalm 34:21–22

Allow five to six minutes for study and call for reports of the first three groups.

Place the second strip poster on the wall and call for group 4 and group 5 to report.

Give the Truth a Personal Focus

Distribute paper and pencils to members. Remind them that 34:3 suggests that personal testimonies can be a way of encouraging other believers. Ask members to write their own brief testimony of the way God delivered them in times of trouble. They may begin with something like: "O magnify the Lord with me, and let us exalt his name together for . . ." Allow time for work, and then call on several to read what they have written. Close by giving members an opportunity to offer sentences prayers to express their gratitude for God's deliverance in times of trouble.

Praising God Who Knows and Cares

Basic Passage: Psalm 139
Focal Passages: Psalm 139:1–14, 23–24

With reverent awe, the psalmist meditated on the God who knew him completely, whose presence was with him wherever he was, who shaped him from before birth, and before whom his whole life was lived out. The superscription indicates that the psalm was used in public worship, set to music as part of the Davidic collection.

▶ ▶ ▶ ▶ ▶ ▶ ▶ ▶ ▶ **Study Aim:** *To evaluate personal experience with God in light of the personal experience reflected in Psalm 139*

STUDYING THE BIBLE

LESSON OUTLINE
I. God Knows Me (Ps. 139:1–6)
  1. God's knowledge of me (Ps. 139:1–4)
  2. God's hand laid on me (Ps. 139:5)
  3. Beyond human knowledge (Ps. 139:6)
II. God Is with Me (Ps. 139:7–12
  1. God's inescapable presence (Ps. 139:7–8)
  2. Held by God's hand (Ps. 139:9–10)
  3. With Him in the darkness (Ps. 139:11–12)
III. God Created Me (Ps. 139:13–18)
  1. Created before birth (Ps. 139:13–16)
  2. God's wondrous ways (Ps. 139:17–18)
IV. God Hears My Prayers (Ps. 139:19–24)
  1. Condemnation of God's enemies (Ps. 139:19–22)
  2. Prayer for understanding and guidance (Ps. 139:23–24)

The Lord knew the psalmist and everything about him (vv. 1–4). God surrounded him and laid His hand on him (v. 5). God's ways are beyond human understanding (v. 6). Since God is everywhere, His presence is inescapable (vv. 7–8). No matter where the psalmist might travel, the hand of the Lord held him (vv. 9–10). No night was so dark but that God was with the psalmist in the darkness (vv. 11–12). God created him from his mother's womb (vv. 13–16). God's thoughts are precious and as numerous as sand (vv. 17–18). Those who opposed God would be destroyed (vv. 19–22). The psalmist prayed for the Lord's vindication and guidance (vv. 23–24).

I. God Knows Me (Ps. 139:1–6)
1. God's knowledge of me (vv. 1–4)
   1 O Lord, thou hast searched me, and known me.

The psalmist affirmed that the Lord knew him. The fact that he addressed God in prayer shows also that he knew God. He did not know God in so perfect a way as God knew him. He stood in awe before the mystery of God. Still he dared to address God in prayer. The Bible writers did not make impersonal and abstract statements about God. Rather they had a personal faith expressed in prayer and praise to God.

2 Thou knowest my downsitting and mine uprising, thou understandest my thought afar off.

3 Thou compassest my path and my lying down, and art acquainted with all my ways.

4 For there is not a word in my tongue, but, lo, O Lord, thou knowest it altogether.

Not only did the Lord know the psalmist, but He also knew everything about him. God was aware of every detail of his daily routine. For example, God knew when he sat down and when he rose up. God knew the path he took and when he lay down to rest. God knew not only everything he did but also everything he thought. God knew what he would say even before he said it.

2. God's hand laid on me (v. 5)

5 Thou hast beset me behind and before, and laid thine hand upon me.

The word *beset* is used elsewhere in the Old Testament to describe laying siege to a city. Just as an army may lay siege to a city by surrounding it, so God is "all around me on every side" (GNB). Only the context of the entire psalm can determine how the psalmist felt about God surrounding him and laying His hand on him. During his complaints against his sufferings, Job complained of God's hand being laid heavy on him (see Job 10:8). However, later references in Psalm 139 seem to call for a positive interpretation of verse 5. This sees God's hand on him like the hand of a loving father. Sometimes a father's hand is laid on his children to lead or to discipline, but his hand is also to protect, encourage, or help. (See further on v. 10.)

3. Beyond human understanding (v. 6)

6 Such knowledge is too wonderful for me; it is high, I cannot attain unto it.

The psalmist confessed that his awareness of God's knowledge of him left him mentally exhausted. He could not comprehend such knowledge. Fortunately, we do not have to understand God in order to trust Him and His loving care. People who are closest to God are most aware of how little they comprehend of the mystery of God and His ways (see Isa. 55:9; Rom. 11:33).

II. God Is with Me (Ps. 139:7–12)

1. God's inescapable presence (vv. 7–8)

7 Whither shall I go from thy spirit? or whither shall I flee from thy presence?

Like many verses in Hebrew poetry, the two lines of verse 7 repeat the same question using slightly different words. He was asking if he could go any place where God was not present also. Was the psalmist trying to escape from God's presence as Jonah tried to do? The answer to the psalmist's question in verses 8–12 seems to show that the psalmist was not trying to escape from God. He was glorying in the fact that God's presence was with him wherever he was.

8 If I ascend up into heaven, thou art there: if I make my bed in hell, behold, thou art there.

Several words are translated "hell" in the King James Version. This may cause some confusion for the reader. Sometimes "hell" translates a word that refers only to the realm of the dead, as in Psalm 139. At other times, the word refers to the place of punishment. One characteristic of the latter use of "hell" is that God is not there.

The Christian doctrine of eternal life was a matter of divine revelation. During early stages of revelation, people of faith had only a dim awareness of what we know to be the full glory of life after death. Psalm 139:8 is a glint of light as the psalmist dared to believe that God would be with him beyond death itself.

2. Held by God's hand (vv. 9–10)

9 If I take the wings of the morning, and dwell in the uttermost parts of the sea;

10 Even there shall thy hand lead me, and thy right hand shall hold me.

Verse 9 is another vivid example of the Lord's abiding presence. The psalmist imagined going as far as possible toward the east where the sun rose. He also imagined going far to the west beyond the Mediterranean Sea. Most translators think the wording in Hebrew refers to the "far side of the sea" (NIV).

Verse 10 is another reference to God's hand. The reference in verse 5 may be ambiguous, but the meaning of verse 10 is positive. God's hand led him and held him. These are pictures of loving guidance and protection. This testimony is similar to Psalm 73:23–24, "I am continually with thee: thou hast holden me by my right hand. Thou shalt guide me with thy counsel, and afterward receive me to glory."

3. With Him in the darkness (vv. 11–12)

11 If I say, Surely the darkness shall cover me even the night shall be light about me.

12 Yea, the darkness hideth not from thee; but the night shineth as the day: the darkness and the light are both alike to thee.

Some Bible students interpret these verses as if the psalmist was trying to hide from God. If so, the point is that he discovered that no darkness was deep enough to escape the presence of God. More likely, however, the psalmist was using the darkness as a symbol of troubles, which are dark periods of one's life. If that was his meaning, the point in verses 11–12 is that no night is so dark but that the Lord's sustaining presence pierces through the darkness like light.

III. God Created Me (Ps. 139:13–18)
1. Created before birth (vv. 13–16)

13 For thou hast possessed my reins: thou hast covered me in

my mother's womb.

Another translation of verse 13 is, "For you created my inmost being; you knit me together in my mother's womb" (NIV). The reason the Lord knew everything about the psalmist (vv. 1–6) was that God created him within his mother's womb. By the same token, God whose presence was always with him was with him even before his birth. Verses 13–16 show that the psalmist believed that God's creative work includes the creation of new life within the womb.

14 I will praise thee; for I am fearfully and wonderfully made: marvellous are thy works; and that my soul knoweth right well.

The psalmist's response to this reality was to praise God his Creator and the giver of life. The Old Testament idea of creation makes clear that our whole existence belongs not to ourselves, but to the God who created us for Himself. Apart from God, life has no explanation or purpose. When we contemplate God's grace, wisdom, and power in our creation, we bow in praise to Him.

Verse 15 makes the same point as verse 13 except that the heart of the earth signifies the mother's womb. Verse 16 is not easy to translate or understand, but the thought seems to be that God wrote the psalmist's name in the book of the living, even before he was born.

2. God's wondrous ways (vv. 17–18). Verses 17–18 express a similar sentiment to verse 6. The psalmist contemplated the thoughts of God, which seemed as numerous as the sand. As he stood in awe before the infinite wisdom, grace, and power of God, he clung in trust to the assurance that this God of the universe was still with him.

IV. God Hears My Prayers (Ps. 139:19–24)

1. Condemnation of God's enemies (vv. 19–22). Verses 19–22 were not a call for God to take vengeance on the enemies of the psalmist. Instead he was writing of those whose actions showed them to be enemies of God. The psalmist asked that God would deal with them as they deserved.

2. Prayer for understanding and guidance (vv. 23–24)

23 Search me, O God, and know my heart: try me, and know my thoughts:

24 And see if there be any wicked way in me, and lead me in the way everlasting.

The words "wicked way" sometimes denote idolatry. Some Bible students think that the psalmist had been accused of idol worship. This would explain the tone of this prayer. The psalmist was not claiming to be perfect, but he wanted God and others to know that he had not turned from God to idols. In any case, verses 23–24a reflect not arrogant pride but a humble awareness that God knows all about us. The psalmist threw himself in trust on the loving God who knows but who also understands and forgives. The last part of verse 24 is a prayer that God would guide the steps of the psalmist in the right way, the way that leads to life, even to life everlasting.

1. God knows where we are. Have you ever felt that God has moved off and left no forwarding address? If so, it isn't because He has moved from us but because we have moved from Him. In some "dry spell" of life when the burdens have lain heavily upon you, have you felt God doesn't know your need or, if He does, He just doesn't care? Many of us have felt that way, and so did many of the psalmists. But this psalmist knows full well that God knows all about him and his needs (vv. 1-4) and he isn't a bit uncomfortable with that.

Paul Harvey once told about a criminal who used acid to burn away his fingerprints so that he could carry on his thievery without being caught. But then he was easily caught because he was the only thief who left no fingerprints behind! With or without fingerprints, without dental records, or without any distinguishing marks, God knows us and more—He knows everything about us.

Are you uncomfortable with this?

2. The hands of God. With a good concordance, run the references on the hands of God and the hands of Jesus. God had laid His holy hands on this psalmist and he rejoices in it (v. 5).

We have experienced the same thing. In daily life, or in some acute emergency, we have been aware of His presence with us and of His hands upon us.

One of the best-known preachers of history had such an experience. English preacher George Whitefield (Whit-field) was on his way from America to England in 1731. The trip had been dangerous for months and the crew sensed impending disaster. In his journal Whitefield wrote: "Our allowance of water is just one pint a day, our sails are exceedingly thin, and some of them last night were split. No one knows where we are, but God does and that is sufficient."

3. A pilot's passenger. A young pilot was making his solo flight when he got into serious trouble. Finally, after a difficult struggle, he landed the plane safely. Filling in his log, in the place where it asked for passengers, the young airman wrote "God."[1]

Like the pilot, the psalmist knew that even in the heavens high above the earth, God was still with him.

4. God is with us in the darkness. There can be something fearful about the darkness. Walking on a dark city street, or walking into a darkened home or building, can cause the hair on the back of our necks to bristle.

English Baptist pastor Alexander Maclaren (1826–1910), tells about a frightening experience he had as a teenage boy that left a lasting impression. He took a job in town that required his walking through a thick forest, reported to be haunted, in order to get home. And to compound his fear of the woods, he had to walk through it at night.

One night he entered the woods and, hearing a noise some distance behind him, he picked up the pace. And the sound of feet walking on leaves behind him picked up its pace. In a little while, he began to run, and the noise coming after him sounded as though someone was running. Alexander was nearly scared out of his wits when, suddenly, from behind him he heard someone call, "Alexander! Alexander!" and then he recognized the voice of his father.

Not even the darkness hides us from God, the psalmist says. The darkness of the night, or the black darkness of a personal problem, will not cut us off from God (vv. 11–12). Let us comfort ourselves with the promise, therefore, that "even the night shall be light about me, Yea, the darkness hideth not from Thee."

5. People not numbers. A census taker stopped at a home and asked the mother, "How many children do you have?" She began to name them: "There's Mary, Bob, Jim . . ."

"No, lady, not the names, the numbers." Curtly she replied, "Sir, they do not have numbers, they have names!"

The Bible says that Jesus called His own sheep by name (John 10:3). The psalmist recognized this personal relationship we have with God and states it in verses 13–16. Even in the womb, God knows us and He knows our name. Therein lies the grave sin of abortion.

TEACHING THE BIBLE

▶ *Main Idea:* Understanding that God knows and cares helps us through difficult experiences.
▶ *Suggested Teaching Aim:* To lead adults to describe how the psalmist praised God for knowing and caring about him, and to describe the closeness of our relationship with Him.

A TEACHING OUTLINE

1. Use an illustration to introduce the Bible study.
2. Use a series of questions to guide the Bible study.
3. Use the How to Become a Christian feature to apply the lesson.

Introduce the Bible Study

Use "God knows where we are" from "Applying the Bible" to introduce the session.

Search for Biblical Truth

Down the left side of a chalkboard or a large sheet of paper write: What? How? Where? Why? Ask members to open their Bibles to Psalm 139:1–5. Ask: What do these verses tell us that God knows about us? Let members mention these and list them opposite the word What? (Daily routine, when he sat down and got up, path, and when he rested, everything he thought, surrounded him.) Ask: According to 139:6, what was the psalmist's reaction to this great knowledge? (Too wonderful.)

Ask members to look at 139:7–8. Use the comments on these verses in "Studying the Bible" to explain how *hell* is used in this verse. Ask: How can God be with us in both heaven and hell? Write answers opposite the word *How*? What is the significance of this fact? (Early belief that God was with believers after death.)

Ask members to look at 139:9–12. Ask: According to these verses, where is God's presence with us? (As far east and west as we can go; in deepest darkness.) Write members' answer opposite *Where*?

Ask members to look at 139:13–14. Ask, Why is God with us always? (He created us.) Write this opposite Why?

Explain the meaning of the word reins in 139:13. Ask: What is the significance of this verse in explaining the meaning of life? (Many meanings but consider: Apart from God, life has no purpose.)

Ask a volunteer to read aloud 139:23–24. Using the information in "Studying the Bible," explain the possible reference to idolatry and the psalmist's desire to stand before God and be led to life everlasting.

Give the Truth a Personal Focus

Ask, How many of your activities this past week would you be uncomfortable in sharing with the class? Did you have any thoughts this past week that you would be uncomfortable in sharing with the class?

Assure members that you are not going to ask them to reveal these actions and thoughts, but point out that God knows everything we did and thought this past week. Ask: Does this fact encourage you or frighten you? What did this knowledge do for the psalmist? (Encouraged him because he had been accused of something he had not done.) Point out that the wonderful side of knowing that God understands all about us is that when others accuse us of doing something we did not do, God knows all of the details; He knows we are in the right.

Point out that on the other side, we cannot fool God because He does know if we are genuine in our response to Him.

Ask members to bow their heads and consider how close they are to God as you read 139:23–24. Offer peace and hope to those who have been misunderstood; offer forgiveness to those in whom God does find some "wicked way."

If you have members who are not Christians, you may want to turn to the front of the book and share the "How to Become a Christian" feature.

---

1. Adapted from *Proclaim* (July–September, 1976).

Trust in God

Basic Passage: Psalm 40
Focal Passages: Psalm 40:1–5, 9–11, 16–17

P salm 40 has two distinct parts. Verses 1–10 constitute a testimony of deliverance and a call for patient trust in God. Verses
11–17 contain a prayer for God's grace and help in a current crisis. Most of Psalm 40:13–17 appears also in Psalm 70.

▶ ▶ ▶ ▶ **Study Aim:** *To exercise patient trust in God during times of
trouble*

STUDYING THE BIBLE

LESSON OUTLINE
  I. A Testimony of Deliverance (Ps. 40:1–10)
     1. Patient trust and divine deliverance (Ps. 40:1–2)
     2. Influencing others to trust in God (Ps. 40:3–5)
     3. Offering joyous obedience (Ps. 40:6–8)
     4. Bearing glad testimony (Ps. 40:9–10)
  II. A Prayer for Help (Ps. 40:11–17)
     1. Asking for God's grace and help (Ps. 40:11–13)
     2. Let the wicked be confounded (Ps. 40:14–15)
     3. Let the righteous magnify the Lord (Ps. 40:16)
     4. Humble trust in the Lord (Ps. 40:17)

The psalmist testified how the Lord responded to his patient trust
by delivering him from a terrible situation (vv. 1–2). He sang a new
song of praise that he expected to lead others to the blesssedness of
trusting in the Lord, whose deliverances of His people were too many
to number (vv. 3–5). The psalmist had learned that the Lord wanted
obedience to His will, rather than sacrifices (vv. 6–8). Thus, in the congregation he bore testimony to the righteousness, faithfulness, salvation, lovingkindness, and truth of God (vv. 9–10). He prayed for God's
grace and help as he faced a new crisis and his own sins (vv. 11–13).
He asked God to confound those who threatened him and mocked him
and God (vv. 14–15). He interceded that God's people might magnify
His name (v. 16). He expressed his own humble trust as he asked God
to hasten to help him (v. 17).

I. A Testimony of Deliverance
(Ps. 40:1–10)
1. Patient trust and divine deliverance (vv. 1–2)
     **1 I waited patiently for the Lord; and he inclined unto me, and
     heard my cry.**
     **2 He brought me up also out of an horrible pit, out of the miry
     clay, and set my feet upon a rock, and established my goings.**
The psalmist testified how God had delivered him from a terrible

situation. Many Bible students think that the "horrible pit" and "miry clay" describe a sickness or situation in which the psalmist was at death's door. He did not go into details about his plight, but it was something that was comparable to being in a horrible pit and miry clay. The "miry clay" was like quicksand, into which he continued to sink ever deeper. Perhaps it is just as well that we don't know exactly what was happening to him. This enables us to identify our own crises with his description in verse 2.

In this situation, the psalmist cried out to the Lord for help. Apparently the deliverance didn't come right away, for the psalmist said that he "waited patiently" for the Lord. Eventually, however, the Lord heard and answered the psalmist's prayer of patient trust. Verse 2 describes both the negative and positive aspects of the Lord's deliverance. The Lord lifted him out of the horrible pit and miry clay. The Lord also set his feet on a rock and thus provided a firm foundation for his life.

Over the years, I have heard many people give a similar testimony. They describe a terrible situation through which they are passing or have passed. They testify that they could not have survived without the Lord's help. Sometimes the help involved removal of the trouble; often the help involved grace and strength to endure the trouble (see comments on v. 17).

2. Influencing others to trust in God (vv. 3–5)

3 And he hath put a new song in my mouth, even praise unto our God: many shall see it, and fear, and shall trust in the Lord.

If we will let Him, God teaches us many lessons in the school of life, especially in the class called "trouble." Going through a time of trouble makes any person reflect on life and its meaning. Those of us who believe

Statuette of Baal, the Canaanite weather god, from Minet-el-Beida (15th–14th century B.C.) *Biblical Illustrator* 482/3.

in God come through trouble with a new appreciation of life as the fragile gift of God. When life and health are threatened and then saved or restored, people of faith have a new awareness of what is important. The psalmist emerged from his trouble with a new song of praise to God. This may mean that he composed this psalm as a new song of praise. Or it may mean that he sang the familiar words of hymns of praise with a new sense of reality and praise to God. His whole life was renewed, and he expressed it in songs of praise to God. He also expected his songs of praise and testimony to be used by God to lead others to see God, themselves, and life in a new way. As a result, they would fear the Lord and trust Him. Thus the psalmist hoped that his testimony of deliverance through patient trust would lead others to trust the Lord for themselves.

4 Blessed is that man that maketh the Lord his trust, and respecteth not the proud, nor such as turn aside to lies.

Using the form of a Beatitude (see Ps. 1:1; Matt. 5:3–12), the psalmist pronounced a blessing on those who trusted in the Lord. He contrasted them with those who put their trust in "lies." Most Bible students think that the "lies" referred to trust in false gods, rather than in the true and living God. Those who put their trust in false gods are seduced by lies. Many people in every generation allow themselves to be deceived into trusting something other than the God who made them.

5 Many, O Lord my God, are thy wonderful works which thou hast done, and thy thoughts which are to us-ward: they cannot be reckoned up in order unto thee: if I would declare and speak of them, they are more than can be numbered.

The psalmist acknowledged that the Lord had blessed and delivered many people, not just him. As he thanked God for his personal deliverance, he also praised God for His wonderful works done on behalf of all His people. These included individual blessings and deliverances, but they also included acts of divine deliverance and blessing on Israel as a whole. Thus verse 5 echoes a typical Old Testament theme: the grateful remembrance of God's mighty acts on behalf of His people. (For example, that is the theme of Ps. 105, which we studied on July 14.) The psalmist was amazed when he tried to recount the many instances of divine deliverance, which were too numerous to count.

3. Offering joyous obedience (vv. 6–8). A typical response to such divine deliverance was to offer a sacrifice in the temple. However, the Lord had opened the psalmist's ears to recognize what so many of the prophets declared: the Lord wants obedience, not sacrifices (v. 6; see 1 Sam. 15:22; Isa. 1:11–17; Hos. 6:6; Amos 5:21–24; Mic. 6:6–8). A book—probably the law of God—called the psalmist to obedience to God (v. 7). Thus the psalmist delighted in doing God's will and obeying the law written within his heart (v. 8).

4. Bearing glad testimony (vv. 9–10)

9 I have preached righteousness in the great congregation: lo, I have not refrained my lips, O Lord, thou knowest.

10 I have not hid thy righteousness within my heart; I have declared thy faithfulness and thy salvation: I have not concealed thy lovingkindness and thy truth from the great congregation.

In his prayer to God, the psalmist noted that he had not kept silent about what God had done for Him and about how great God is. He had spoken boldly in the great congregation, the people who gathered to worship the Lord. The words used in verses 9–10 are the words used in the Old Testament to describe who God is and what He is like. The psalmist bore witness to God's righteousness, faithfulness, salvation, lovingkindness, and truth. Each of these powerful words focuses on some facet of the greatness of our God.

Each believer is a witness of God and His grace. We need to give our testimony of God's grace and help in our own lives. We need to boldly tell all who will hear. Certainly we need to bear witness within our own class and congregation. When others hear such testimonies, many are led to trust and praise God.

II. A Prayer for Help (Ps. 40:11–17)

1. Asking for God's grace and help (vv. 11–13)

11 Withhold not thou thy tender mercies from me, O Lord: let

thy lovingkindness and thy truth continually preserve me.

Verse 11 is a transition verse. The psalmist testified to God's deliverance in a past time of trouble in verses 1–10. In verse 11, he asked that the Lord's grace would continually sustain and preserve him. This prayer is linked to a prayer for grace and help in a current crisis, which is described in verse 12. The psalmist declared that he was surrounded by innumerable troubles and overwhelmed by his own iniquities (v. 12). He faced this new crisis as he had faced the earlier one described in verse 2. He prayed for the Lord to come quickly to help him (v. 13).

2. Let the wicked be confounded (vv. 14–15). Very likely, his current crisis involved danger from enemies. At any rate, in verse 14 he asked God to confound those who threatened him. Verse 15 describes their mocking cries against the psalmist and against God. The psalmist prayed that the Lord would put to shame those who sought to shame him.

3. Let the righteous magnify the Lord (v. 16)

16 Let all those that seek thee rejoice and be glad in thee: let such as love thy salvation say continually, The Lord be magnified.

To the psalmist's credit, he focused his prayer beyond his own personal crisis. He interceded on behalf of all God's people. Remembering the lesson he had learned from his earlier deliverance, he prayed that people of faith would find their highest joy in the Lord. Closely related is the prayer that people of faith would praise and testify to the Lord by saying, "Let the Lord be magnified."

4. Humble trust in the Lord (v. 17)

17 But I am poor and needy; yet the Lord thinketh upon me: thou art my help and my deliverer; make no tarrying, O my God.

The psalmist recognized that he was poor and needy in the sight of the Lord. This kind of humble trust is what Jesus meant when He said, "Blessed are the poor in spirit" (Matt. 5:3). The psalmist saw himself as spiritually poverty-stricken. Yet he was encouraged by faith that the Lord knew him and his situation, and cared about him. Thus he affirmed his trust in the Lord as his help and deliverer. He closed with a prayer that the Lord his God would hasten to his aid.

He was in the kind of situation that every believer encounters at times in life. He was in trouble. He had prayed in faith that the Lord would help him. He was waiting for and asking for deliverance. We don't know whether the psalmist was delivered from this trouble as he was from the one described in verses 1–2. We do know that God heard and answered his prayer, which sometimes doesn't include being delivered from a troubling situation but being strengthened to endure with patient trust. Most people of faith can testify of times when the Lord delivered them from bad situations, just as they had asked Him to do. We also can testify how the Lord often provided grace and strength to endure faithfully through a time of trouble.

APPLYING THE BIBLE

1. Easy to trust when all goes well. When everything in our life is moving along pleasantly, it is easy to trust God and have the assurance that all will turn out well. But when the darkness comes and the way is unclear and the burdens are heavy, trusting God is another matter. We want to move against the thing that burdens us rather than wait "patiently for the Lord" (v. 1) as the psalmist instructs us.

It is just at this point that the way Jesus handled trials is in contrast with how we handle them.

When Satan tempted Jesus to turn stones into bread in the wilderness, Jesus refused, saying: "Man shall not live by bread alone." When He sat with the Samaritan woman, tired and weary from His journey, He showed love and compassion for the adulterous woman (John 4). When He was reviled, He did not revile in return. And in the last hours of His life, He forgave and prayed for His tormentors.

This psalmist is learning to trust God patiently and not run ahead of Him (vv. 1–4). In our burdens and cares, we must not run ahead of God.

2. The song of the one delivered. The psalmist had been delivered from some terrible crisis (v. 2). Or perhaps, it was the removal of the guilt of sin he had committed. Anyway, he was safe for he had been delivered, and he sang a song of rejoicing in his heart.

Singing has marked believers in every era of time—singing in times of joy and times of crisis. The magnificent music of the slaves in the Old South developed as an escape vent for their frustrations and sorrows. From them and their singing their way from sadness to joy, we can learn a great lesson.

An anonymous poet has described the trust we should have in our loving Lord in these four simple lines: "Let me like a little sparrow/Trust Him where I cannot see,/In the sunshine or the shadow,/Singing He will care for me."

3. The lost word. George Buttrick, who was an Episcopal rector in New York City, said that *obedience* is a lost word in our culture. Discussing obedience in his book *Don't Sleep Through the Revolution*, Paul S. Rees says that "Christian obedience is surrender to God's will as revealed in Jesus Christ and set out in Holy Scripture."[1]

Rees adds that Christian obedience is not blind acquiescence to blind fate; rather it is joyous, full-heart commitment to our gentle Savior. It is the product of repentance from sin and saving faith in Jesus Christ. It springs to life when our pride is slain with Jesus on the cross and our arrogant will has been submitted to the Lordship of Jesus.

David Livingstone, who spent three decades as a missionary physician in Africa, wrote beautifully about Christian obedience near the end of his life: "Christ is the greatest Master I have ever known. If there is anyone greater, I do not know him. Jesus Christ is the only Master supremely worth serving. He is the only ideal that never loses its inspiration. . . . We go forth in His name, in His power, in His Spirit, to serve Him.[2]

4. The one thing we can't live without. There are many things we think we need, and some are certainly valid needs. But there is one thing without which we cannot live well and joyously: grace! In our lesson the psalmist, knowing this, prayed for grace to cover and surround him (vv. 11–13). What his crisis was we do not know, but we do know that his need for forgiveness was one of them (v. 12).

As a boy, I learned this lesson the hard way, as have most of us. I stole some money from an Indian girl who lived on the Osage reservation near our home and bought a cap pistol for myself. I still have the picture of myself as a ten-year-old boy, with a bandanna around my neck, astride a stick horse, proudly displaying my cap pistol bought with stolen money.

Months went by and the Holy Spirit began to convict me of my sin. One day I stood on the back porch and flung the dreaded thing, that had became like a serpent to me, across the fence and into the field. "I am done with it," I said to myself. When the field was plowed, the pistol was turned under, and I rejoiced. But, lo and behold, when we next plowed the field the pistol was turned up and there it lay on top of the ground hissing at me, "You are not done with me yet!"

I have since tried to find the girl and make restitution to her, as the Scriptures teach, but to no avail. But I did find forgiveness for my sin through the grace of our Lord Jesus.

"It's such a small thing," you say. No, it was a sin, and God does not measure sin as little or big. It is all an act of disobedience, and the only answer to it is the grace of God.

Since that day long ago, I have said and done other things that violate the divine standard. But the answer to them has been the same answer I discovered as a boy: grace!

Have you discovered it to cover your sins?

TEACHING THE BIBLE

▶ *Main Idea*: God's deliverance of us in the past demonstrates that He will care for us in the present.

▶ *Suggested Teaching Aim:* To lead adults to determine how God cared for the psalmist, and to apply His grace to a current crisis they are going through.

A TEACHING OUTLINE

1. Use an illustration to introduce the session.

2. Use a new room arrangement to indicate variety.

3. Use a brief lecture and discussion questions to guide the Bible study through each verse on the Focal Passage.

4. Use reflection to help members apply the lesson.

Introduce the Bible Study

Use "The one thing we can't live without" from "Applying the Bible" to introduce the session.

Search for Biblical Truth

IN ADVANCE, make a poster with the following words from "Studying the Bible:" "If we will let Him, God teaches us many lessons in the school of life, especially in the class called 'trouble.'" Place this on the focal wall.

If possible, place half the chairs on one side of the room and half on the other, facing each other. Leave a space between them. Place one of the following posters over each side: "I. A Testimony of Deliverance (Ps. 40:1–10)"; "II. A Prayer for Help (Ps. 40:11–17)."

IN ADVANCE, copy the eight sentences in the first introductory paragraph under "Studying the Bible" on eight small strips of paper. (Number the strips 1–8 so readers will know what order they are to read.) Tape the four strips that relate to 40:1–10 to chairs on the "Testimony" side; tape the other four to chairs on the "Prayer" side. Ask members to read the strips to survey the chapter.

Call for a volunteer from the "Testimony" side to read 40:1–2. Explain "miry clay" and why the psalmist waited patiently.

DISCUSS: What do you do when deliverance does not come as quickly as you would like for it to come?

Call for a volunteer from the "Testimony" side to read 40:3. Refer to the "Lessons" poster on the wall and explain the reference to "new song."

DISCUSS: What new understanding have you gained as a result of trouble or conflict?

Call for a volunteer from the "Testimony" side to read 40:4-5. Explain *Beatitude* and "lies."

DISCUSS: What wonderful works has God performed in your life? Did you deserve any of them?

Call for a volunteer from the "Testimony" side to read 40:9–10. Explain "great congregation" and "hid thy righteousness." Point out that the psalmist bore witness to God's righteousness, faithfulness, salvation, lovingkindness, and truth.

DISCUSS: How can you witness to God's grace this week?

Call for a volunteer from the "Prayer" side to read 40:11. Point out that the verse is a transition between the testimony and the prayer.

DISCUSS: How does God's past leading help you currently?

Call for a volunteer from the "Prayer" side to read 40:16. Point out that the psalmist prayed for others as he prayed for himself.

DISCUSS: Do we ever have a right to pray just for ourselves in a time of crisis or should our prayers always include those who do not know how to pray for themselves?

Call for a volunteer from the "Prayer" side to read 40:17. Point out the humble trust the psalmist displayed.

DISCUSS: Would you agree with this statement: "God hears and answers all our prayers, but sometimes the answer doesn't include being delivered from a troubling situation but being strengthened to endure with patient trust."

Give the Truth a Personal Focus

Ask members to bow their heads and in a moment of silence identify a current crisis in their lives in which they need to apply God's grace. Read again the "Lesson" poster and urge them to exercise patient trust in God during times of trouble. Close in a prayer that all will know God's loving grace.

---

1. Paul S. Rees, *Don't Sleep Through the Revolution* (Waco, Tex.: Word Books, 1969), 55.
2. Ibid., 57–58.

Obey God's Laws

Basic Passages: Psalm 119:1–16, 45, 105, 129–130
Focal Passages: Psalm 119:1–16, 45, 105, 129–130

P salm 119 is the longest psalm and the longest chapter in the Bible. The form of Psalm 119 is an alphabetic acrostic; that is, each of its stanzas begins with a different letter in the Hebrew alphabet, and each line within a stanza begins with the same letter. For example, each line in verses 1–8 begins with the Hebrew letter *aleph*, which is comparable to the letter *a* in English. Psalm 119 is a prayerful meditation on the law of God. The passages selected for study in this lesson focus on the blessedness and benefits of obeying God's law.

 **Study Aim:** *To testify of the benefits of studying and following God's Word*

STUDYING THE BIBLE

LESSON OUTLINE
 I. Blessedness of Obeying God's Law (Ps. 119:1–8)
  1. The fact of blessedness (Ps. 119:1–3)
  2. Prayer (Ps. 119:4–6)
  3. Commitment (Ps. 119:7–8)
 II. Benefits of Obeying God's Law (Ps. 119:9–16, 45, 105, 129–130)
  1. Overcoming temptation (Ps. 119:9–11)
  2. True riches (Ps. 119:12–16)
  3. Freedom (Ps. 119:45)
  4. Guidance (Ps. 119:105)
  5. Understanding (Ps. 119:129–130)

Those who keep God's Word are blessed (vv. 1–3). The psalmist prayed that he might keep God's statutes (vv. 4–6). He committed himself to praise God by obeying God's law (vv. 7–8). He testified that hiding God's Word in our hearts enables us to overcome temptation (vv. 9–11). He found joy in God's Word comparable to the joy of having great riches (vv. 12–16). He found freedom in obeying God's Word (v. 45). He found guidance for knowing and doing God's will, since the Word was like a light on his path (v. 105). He testified that God's Word provided understanding, even for the simple (vv. 129–130).

I. Blessedness of Obeying God's Law (Ps. 119:1–8)

1. The fact of blessedness (vv. 1–3)
   1 Blessed are the undefiled in the way, who walk in the law of the Lord.
   2 Blessed are they that keep his testimonies, and that seek him with the whole heart.

3 They also do no iniquity: they walk in his ways.

The psalm begins like Psalm 1, with a declaration of the blessedness of those who walk in the way of the Lord. Psalm 119 emphasizes that the way of the Lord is expressed in His law. As used here, the word "law" refers to more than a set of rules. It refers to the revealed will of God for how His people are to live: commandments, instructions, examples, and so forth. The Old Testament people of faith did not look on the law as a heavy burden. Those who later made it into a heavy burden by adding their own rigid traditions did not accurately express how writers of the Old Testament felt about God's law (see Matt. 23:4).

One of the characteristics of Psalm 119 is the large number of words that the psalmist used to describe God's law or Word. Verse 1, for example, uses "way"; and verse 2 uses "testimonies." Later in the psalm, a number of other words were used: "commandments," "statutes," "precepts," "word," and "judgments." Each of these has a slightly different emphasis, but the psalmist used all these words to describe God's Word.

Just as the psalm uses a variety of words to describe God's Word, it also uses a variety of expressions to describe how people of faith respond to God's Word. For example, the word "walk" is used in verses 1 and 3 to stress that living by God's Word is a way of life. The words "undefiled" (v. 1) and "no iniquity" (v. 3) describe the difference that obeying God's law makes in one's life. The word "keep" denotes treasuring the Word and obeying it. The clause "seek him with the whole heart" shows that responding to the Word of God is seen as responding to God, whose Word it is. Those who live by the Word of God can do so only as they seek the Lord Himself with all their heart.

2. Prayer (vv. 4–6)

4 Thou hast commanded us to keep thy precepts diligently.

5 O that my ways were directed to keep thy statutes!

6 Then shall I not be ashamed, when I have respect unto all thy commandments.

Beginning with verse 4 and continuing through most of the rest of Psalm 119, the psalmist addressed himself directly to the Lord. This underlines the comments about the words "seek him with the whole heart" in verse 2. The psalmist practiced what he preached. After pronouncing the blessedness of the person who obeys God's Word, he prayed that God would enable him to do just that. Recognizing that God had directed him to keep His precepts diligently (v. 4), he prayed that God would direct his ways to keep God's statutes (v. 5). He realized that he could not do this in his own strength. If God would help him keep His commandments, then he would not be ashamed by failing God (v. 6).

3. Commitment (vv. 7–8)

7 I will praise thee with uprightness of heart, when I shall have learned thy righteous judgments.

8 I will keep thy statutes: O forsake me not utterly.

The psalmist spelled out his twofold commitment. For one thing, he would praise the Lord with a life that had been changed by obedience to God's Word. This shows that our lives as well as our voices are to praise the Lord. The second commitment was to keep God's statutes.

Verse 8 closes with the same kind of prayer we saw in last week's lesson in Psalm 40:17. The psalmist recognized the depth of his need and his inclinations to fail God; therefore, he prayed for the Lord's presence never to forsake him.

II. Benefits of Obeying God's Law (Ps. 119:9–16, 45, 105, 129–130)

1. Overcoming temptation (vv. 9–11)

9 Wherewithal shall a young man cleanse his way? by taking heed thereto according to thy word.

Verse 9 reminds us of the Book of Proverbs, which so often addresses its instructions to young men. Those who are young are still forming their basic outlook and approach to life. Many of the immature young fall prey to ways that are destructive in the long run. Thus the question in verse 9 is answered in the same verse. A young man can cleanse his way by taking heed to live according to God's Word.

10 With my whole heart have I sought thee: O let me not wander from thy commandments.

Verse 10 is a testimony of one whose whole heart was committed to seeking the Lord and His will. The psalmist prayed that God would not let him wander from God's commandments. If we are honest, we must confess to being prone to wander. We need to join the psalmist in praying that the Lord will bind our wandering hearts to Him.

11 Thy word have I hid in mine heart, that I might not sin against thee.

This is one of the most familiar verses in Psalm 119, and rightly so. The psalmist put into words a commitment that each of us—young or old—should have made. One guard against falling into sin is to hide God's Word in our heart. This means to memorize pertinent parts of the Bible and to hide them in our minds and hearts. Then when we face trials and temptations, God will bring to mind the strength and direction of His Word for the situation.

2. True riches (vv. 12–16)

12 Blessed art thou, O Lord: teach me thy statutes.

13 With my lips have I declared all the judgments of thy mouth.

14 I have rejoiced in the way of thy testimonies, as much as in all riches.

15 I will meditate in thy precepts, and have respect unto thy ways.

16 I will delight myself in thy statutes: I will not forget thy word.

Notice the five words used to describe God's Word in verses 12–15: "statutes," "judgments," "testimonies," "precepts," and "ways." Also notice the different words that describe the psalmist's actions: "teach me," "declared," "rejoiced," "meditate," "have respect unto," "delight myself," and "not forget." Notice especially the psalmist's high regard for God's Word. Far from considering God's Word to be a set of burdensome rules, he rejoiced in God's Word.

And he compared the law of God to great riches. He had discovered the secret that all people of true faith eventually realize: that life's highest joy is in knowing and serving God and that the revelation of God and His way is more precious than earthly wealth. The most memorable celebration of joy in the riches of God's Word is in Psalm 19:7–10. The psalmist wrote this about God's judgments: "More to be desired are they than gold, yea, than much fine gold: sweeter also than honey and the honeycomb" (Ps. 19:10).

3. Freedom (v. 45)

45 And I will walk at liberty: for I seek thy precepts.

This verse is reminiscent of Jesus' teaching that sin results in slavery and Christian discipleship leads to freedom (see John 8:31–32, 34). Worldly people believe the exact opposite. They are deceived into thinking that selfish sins lead to freedom because each person is allowed to do his own thing. The writer of Psalm 119 had experienced something of what Jesus was teaching. True freedom comes only when people know the God who made them and walk in the way people were intended to live. Those who walk in the ways of sin join the faceless multitude on its way to destruction. Sin doesn't promote freedom; it leads to a plight from which we are helpless to deliver ourselves.

4. Guidance (v. 105)

105 Thy word is a lamp unto my feet, and a light unto my path.

This is another of the most familiar verses in Psalm 119 or in the Bible itself. The Word of God is like light on the path we walk. Without this light, we stumble through life like a person groping about on a dark, moonless night. The Bible is not a book of magic recipes for each situation, but God uses His Word in each of our lives to provide guidance and direction as we seek to know and do His will. Verse 105 goes well with Proverbs 3:5–6: "Trust in the Lord with all thy heart; and lean not unto thine own understanding. In all thy ways acknowledge him, and he shall direct thy paths."

5. Understanding (vv. 129–130)

129 Thy testimonies are wonderful: therefore doth my soul keep them.

130 The entrance of thy words giveth light; it giveth understanding unto the simple.

This passage is similar to verse 105 in mentioning light. However, verse 105 seems to focus on specific direction as we seek the Lord's will, while verse 130 seems to refer to a more general understanding of what life is all about. Every person needs some sense of meaning and purpose in life. People seek meaning in a variety of ways, most of them wrong. The psalmist had found understanding in the wonderful testimonies of the Lord. The entrance of God's words sheds light on the important issues of life. Thus we are faced with the paradox that some of the world's most intelligent and highly trained people seek but never find out what life is all about, while people of much less intelligence and education have found understanding in God's Word.

APPLYING THE BIBLE

1. Some interesting facts about our Bible. Psalm 119 is the longest psalm and the longest chapter in the Bible; the shortest psalm is 117, which is also the middle of the Bible; the middle verse is Psalm 118:8; the longest name in the Bible is "Mahershalalhashbaz" (Isa. 8:1); and the Bible was written using only 6,000 different words, compared to the 20,000 used by Shakespeare.

Also: the shortest verse is John 11:35; all the letters of our English alphabet can be found in Ezra 7:21 except *joy*; the word *and* appears 46,627 times, while the word *Lord* appears 1,855 times; the longest verse is Esther 8:9; and the average word contains but five letters.

The Bible can be read in seventy hours and forty minutes as a minister would read in the pulpit. Reading at an average rate, the Old Testament can be read in fifty-two hours and twenty-two minutes and the New Testament in eighteen hours and twenty minutes. Those who especially love the Psalms can read all one hundred and fifty of them in four hours and twenty-eight minutes. Read the Bible for only twelve minutes a day, and you will read through it in one year.[1]

2. Hitler's comment about the Ten Commandments. Adolph Hitler, the lunatic and dictator who bathed Europe in blood a few decades ago, had no regard for the Scriptures. Hitler once said about the Ten Commandments, "The Ten Commandments have lost their validity. There is no such thing as truth, either in the moral or in the scientific sense." And Hitler gave ample evidence to his belief, murdering millions of innocent people and bringing untold grief to the whole world.

Much to the contrary, the psalmist believed absolutely in God's Word and in the truth it declared. He praised God for His statutes and prayed to be given wisdom to live by them (vv. 1–8).

3. A lesson well learned. When I was a boy, attending Vacation Bible School was a must. Regardless of what had to be done on the farm, we children attended the two-week Bible school year after year. One of the first verses that I learned, after having learned "God is love" in Sunday School, was verse 11 of this chapter: "Thy word have I hid in mine heart, that I might not sin against Thee." I learned that verse well, and practicing it has kept me from many a sin and moral and spiritual failure.

Thank God for my Sunday School and Vacation Bible School teachers, and especially my parents, who taught me God's Word as a child.

4. Finding great treasure. The Bible is a gold mine of wealth and will endure forever. It is the traveler's map through life; the pilot's compass; the pilgrim's staff; the soldier's sword; and the believer's guide. It contains wisdom to teach us; bread to feed us; honey to sweeten us; living water to refresh us; comfort to console us; fire to warm us; and a bed of hope and grace to rest us. Read it to be wise; believe it to be safe; practice it to be holy; and memorize it to grow spiritually. It is more precious than gold: "More to be desired are they than gold" (Ps. 19:10)[2]

As the psalmist points out in our lesson today, to read and love the Word of God is to find an inestimable treasure (vv. 12–16).

5. Lincoln's comfort. Abraham Lincoln found great comfort in the Word of God during America's greatest national crisis. Often, while president, he would arise long before daylight and pour over the Scriptures seeking heaven's guidance.

Joseph R. Sizoo, who years later was pastor of the New York Avenue Presbyterian Church that Lincoln often attended, once told about holding the Bible Lincoln read. His mother had read from that very Bible when he was a child, and she had taught Lincoln to memorize many verses. It was the only possession Lincoln carried from Pigeon Creek, Kentucky, to the Sangamon River in Illinois, and to the White House.

Sizoo wondered, as he held Lincoln's Bible, what had been his favorite passage—or at least one of his favorites. Putting the Bible on its edge, he let it fall open, and it opened to Psalm 37:1, 7: "Fret not thyself because of evildoers." "Rest in the Lord, and wait patiently for Him." The page was well thumbed, testifying that the great president had often turned there for strength and comfort (v. 105, vv. 129–130).[3]

TEACHING THE BIBLE

▶ *Main Idea:* Obeying God's Word demonstrates that believers shall experience lasting benefits.
▶ *Suggested Teaching Aim:* To lead adults to describe the psalmist's description of studying God's Word, and to testify of the benefits of studying and following God's Word.

A TEACHING OUTLINE

1. Use a graffiti wall to introduce the session.
2. Use an antiphonal choir to read the Scripture.
3. Use lecture and group discussion in the Bible study.
4. Use a written testimony to give the Bible truth a personal focus.

Introduce the Bible Study

Keep last week's room arrangement. Use the two groups to read the Scripture antiphonally or responsively. Ask one side to read the first part of each verse ("Blessed are the undefiled in the way") and the other side to read the last part ("who walk in the law of the Lord").

Place a large sheet of paper on the wall and provide markers. As members arrive, ask them to go to the sheet and write their favorite verse from the Psalms. If they do not know the actual reference or wording, assure them that is all right.

Begin the session by reading some of the verses. If you can recognize any from Psalm 119, read them. Point out that Psalm 119 is a psalm about the importance of God's Word.

Search for Biblical Truth

Explain that you will be studying the following sections: all of the first two sections—*aleph* (or A) and *beth* (or B), and parts of *waw* (or W), *nun* (or N), and *pe* (or P). Ask if any members have Bibles that show these divisions?

Ask members to read 119:1–8 as suggested above. Ask members to look at 119:1. Ask: Does this verse remind you of the first verse of another psalm? (It is similar to 1:1.) Point out that these verses describe the blessedness of obeying God's law. Ask members to locate as many words as they can in 119:1–8 that refer to God's Word. (Testimonies, law, ways, precepts, statutes, commandments, judgments.)

Point out that just as the psalm uses a variety of words to describe God's Word, it also uses a variety of expressions to describe how people of faith respond to God's Word. Ask members to see how many of these expressions they can find. (Walk, keep, seek, do no iniquity, have respect, learn thy righteous judgments.)

Point out that from verse 4 on that the psalmist addresses himself directly to the Lord.

Ask members to look at 119:7–8. Ask: According to these verses what is the psalmist's twofold commitment? (Praise the Lord and keep God's statutes.)

DISCUSS: What does it mean for you to "walk in the way of the Lord"? Do you need to make any changes in your life to do this? What do you need to know before you can praise God in a particular situation through which you are going (v. 7)?

On a chalkboard or a large sheet of paper, write: Benefits of Obeying God's Laws. Ask members to read 119:9–16, 45, 105, 129–130 as suggested above. Ask members to examine these verses to find the benefits of obeying God's law. (Members may find several but consider these: overcome temptation, true riches, genuine freedom, guidance, understanding.) Write members' suggestions on the chalkboard or a large sheet of paper.

DISCUSS: How does God bind our wandering hearts to Him (v. 10)? Can you cite an example of a time knowing God's Word kept you from sinning? Which benefit of God's Word is more important to you: freedom (v. 45), guidance (v. 105), or understanding (vv. 129–130)? Why? What difference would it make in your life if you achieved this?

Give the Truth a Personal Focus

Distribute paper and pencils and ask members to write how studying and following God's Word has benefited them. Call on several to read their statements.

---

1. J. B. Fowler, *Illustrating Great Words of the New Testament* (Nashville: Broadman Press, 1991), 161–162 (author unknown).

2. Adapted from *"Faith Prayer and Tract Society League,"* #162 (Grand Rapids, Mich., n.p., n.d.).

3. Adapted from Robert Hastings, *A Word Fitly Spoken* (Nashville: Broadman Press, 1962), 16.

Repent and Confess

Basic Passage: Psalm 51
Focal Passages: Psalm 51:1–13, 17

T he superscription to Psalm 51 says that the historical background
was David's confession of sins after Nathan confronted him with
his guilt concerning Bathsheba (see 2 Sam. 11–12). The psalm
fits well David's remorse when the enormity of his guilt finally broke
through to awaken his conscience

▶ ▶ ▶ ▶ **Study Aim:** *To incorporate in personal prayer life the aspects of
prayer in Psalm 51.*

STUDYING THE BIBLE

LESSON OUTLINE
  I. Praying to God for Forgiveness (Ps. 51:1–12)
    1. Praying to the merciful God (Ps. 51:1–2)
    2. Confessing sins (Ps. 51:3–6)
    3. Seeking cleansing (Ps. 51:7–9)
    4. Asking for renewal (Ps. 51:10–12)
  II. Offering a Changed Life (Ps. 51:13–19)
    1. Converting sinners (Ps. 51:13)
    2. Praising God (Ps. 51:14–15)
    3. Offering oneself (Ps. 51:16–17)
    4. Praying for God's blessing (Ps. 51:18–19)

The psalmist prayed to the God of mercy for cleansing from his
sins (vv. 1–2). Deeply aware of
his sinfulness, he confessed his
sin to God, against whom he
had sinned (vv. 3-6). He
sought cleansing from his sins
(vv. 7–9). He asked for a renewal of spirit based on an
awareness of God's presence
(vv. 10–12). The psalmist committed himself to teach God's
ways so sinners could be converted to Him (v. 13). He
promised to open his mouth in
praise to God (vv. 14–15). He
offered the sacrifice of a broken and contrite heart (vv.
16–17). He prayed for God's
blessings on people who
brought sacrifices of righteousness (vv. 18–19).

Limestone altar. David possibly worshiped at an altar
such as this. The real sacrifice God wants is for us to
feel sorrow deeply in our hearts for sin. *Biblical
Illustrator 57/26-29.*

I. Praying to God for Forgiveness
(Ps. 51:1–12)

1. Praying to the merciful God (vv. 1–2)

1 Have mercy upon me, O God, according to thy lovingkindness: according unto the multitude of thy tender mercies blot out my transgressions.

2 Wash me thoroughly from mine iniquity, and cleanse me from my sin.

Verses 1–2 present the theme of Psalm 51. Notice these three things: (1) words used to describe God, (2) words used to describe sin, and (3) words used to ask for forgiveness.

The words describing God are "mercy," "lovingkindness," and "tender mercies." The psalmist did not base his appeal on his own goodness but on the revealed nature of God as merciful. He did not begin his prayer by reminding God of past good deeds, hoping that this might lessen his guilt. He was too aware of the heavy weight of his own sin and guilt. The broken relationship between him and God completely dominated his thinking. He realized that his only hope lay in God's mercy.

What led the psalmist to dare to expect God to be merciful? The full revelation of God came in Jesus Christ, but God has always been the same. Even in Old Testament times, God sought to make known His mercy and love. The psalmist probably had in mind the revelation of God recorded in Exodus 34:6–7, which is a kind of John 3:16 of the Old Testament. The Lord told Moses His name: "The Lord, The Lord God, merciful and gracious, longsuffering, and abundant in goodness and truth, keeping mercy for thousands, forgiving iniquity and transgression and sin, and that will by no means clear the guilty."

The psalmist used three words to describe his sins. He was not saying that he was guilty of three kinds of sins. His point was that he was a sinner through and through. His sins were a stubborn refusal of God's will ("transgressions"), a perversion of what is right ("iniquity"), and missing the mark ("sin"). He also used three words to describe the forgiveness he sought. He wanted the record of his sins blotted out. He wanted to be washed and cleansed from his sin and guilt.

2. Confessing sins (vv. 3–6)

3 For I acknowledge my transgressions: and my sin is ever before me.

For a long time, David had tried to deceive himself about his sin. He also tried to hide his sin from God and others. When Nathan confronted David with the truth, the structure of his deception collapsed. He realized that he could not hide his sin from God or himself. Thus when he prayed, he said that his sin was ever before him.

4 Against thee, thee only, have I sinned, and done this evil in thy sight: that thou mightest be justified when thou speakest, and be clear when thou judgest.

This verse is sometimes quoted to show that David could not have written Psalm 51. The reason is that David's sins were directly against Bathsheba and Uriah, and his sins had far-reaching deadly effects. How could David write, "Against thee, thee only have I sinned"? However, verse 4 was not intended as a denial of the deadly effects of sin on others. This verse is an exaggerated way of confessing that all sin is ultimately against God. That's what sin is: rebellion against God. Sin has moral and social dimensions, but sin is basically a spiritual matter. Among the worst sins in our world are those directed against people. These sins are wrong because they hurt those whom God loves, and thus they hurt God Himself.

5 Behold, I was shapen in iniquity, and in sin did my mother conceive me.

Verse 5, like verse 4, can be misunderstood. Some have taken it to mean that the sex act by which children are conceived is evil. Others have taken it to mean that sin and guilt are transmitted biologically. The psalmist was not trying to excuse his sins by blaming an inherited sin and guilt. Rather he was using strong language to confess that he was a sinner through and through, and that he lived in a world in which all have sinned against the God who made them.

6 Behold, thou desirest truth in the inward parts: and in the hidden part thou shalt make me to know wisdom.

Verse 6 contrasts with verse 5. Verse 5 is a confession that the psalmist was a sinner through and through. Verse 6 shows what God wanted him to be and indeed what God could make of him. God wants truth, not deception. And God can teach forgiven sinners the wisdom of how to live.

3. Seeking cleansing (vv. 7–9)

7 Purge me with hyssop, and I shall be clean: wash me, and I shall be whiter than snow.

Verses 7–9 continue the prayer for cleansing from verse 2. Hyssop was a plant used in ceremonies of purification and cleansing (see Exod. 12:22). The guilty sinner felt dirty. He yearned for God to cleanse him from the filth of his sins so that he could be whiter than snow (see Isa. 1:18).

8 Make me to hear joy and gladness; that the bones which thou hast broken may rejoice.

During the time when David had tried to hide his sin, he was miserable. Psalm 32:3–4 describes how he felt. He yearned for the joy and gladness of a restored relationship with God (see comments on v. 12).

9 Hide thy face from my sins, and blot out all mine iniquities.

Forgiveness takes place when God sets aside our sin as a barrier to fellowship with Him. Thus, David wanted God to no longer regard his sins as a barrier to such fellowship. As in verse 1, he asked God to blot out the record of his sins.

4. Asking for renewal (vv. 10–12)

10 Create in me a clean heart, O God; and renew a right spirit within me.

The word *create* is the same word used in Genesis 1 of God's creation of all things. The psalmist pleaded for a new heart, something that only God could create. He prayed that God would renew his spirit. He was asking for God to make a profound change in how he thought and felt. He recognized that his own heart and spirit tended to drift from God; he asked for a heart and spirit that could overcome temptation and remain loyal to God.

11 Cast me not away from thy presence; and take not thy holy spirit from me.

The magnitude of his sin caused the psalmist to fear that the joy, comfort, and life-giving presence of God's Spirit might be denied him. He believed the Holy Spirit was still with him; otherwise, he would not have felt divine conviction for his sin. Still he was also aware that sin had interposed a barrier to full fellowship with God. He knew of God's holiness, and he was all too aware of the blackness of his own sin. Therefore, he prayed for God not to withdraw completely from him. In verse 9, he prayed for God to hide His face from his sin; in verse 11, he prayed for God not to hide His face from him—the sinner.

12 Restore unto me the joy of thy salvation; and uphold me with thy free spirit.

When children of God have unconfessed sin in their lives, they lead a joyless existence. This prayer fits well David's experience, but it fits well the experience of any person who allows sin to rob him of the joy of God's salvation. Thus the penitent sinner prayed for a renewal of that joy which flows from communion with God and obedience to His will.

The penitent sinner also asked God to uphold him. The psalmist wanted to serve God with eager willingness and gladness of spirit. But he knew that this did not lie within his own power. Indeed, he lacked motivation, strength, and endurance. Thus, he prayed for God to sustain a willing spirit within him.

II. Offering a Changed Life (Ps. 51:13–19)

1. Converting sinners (v. 13)

13 Then will I teach transgressors thy ways; and sinners shall be converted unto thee.

Up to this point in Psalm 51, the psalmist's full attention was focused on his own relationship with God. Verse 13 shows that he did not practice a self-centered religion. He realized that a right relation with God involved his actions toward others. He was especially sensitive to the plight of those who, like himself, had fallen into sin and needed to turn to God. The penitent sinner vowed that when he was restored to full fellowship with God, he would teach and testify to transgressors so that they might be turned to God.

2. Praising God (vv. 14–15). Asking for deliverance from guilt, the psalmist vowed to sing God's praises (v. 14). Asking God to open his mouth, he promised to lift his voice in praise (v. 15).

3. Offering oneself (vv. 16–17). Verse 16 echoes the prophetic insight of Psalm 40:6 and other passages: God doesn't want burnt offerings.

17 The sacrifices of God are a broken spirit: a broken and a contrite heart, O God, thou wilt not despise.

Before our offerings are acceptable to God, we must first offer ourselves as repentant sinners who become obedient servants of God. David knew that he could go to the house of God and offer all kinds of animal sacrifices. He also knew that none of these sacrifices would please God as long as he was refusing to confess sins. Thus the first sacrifice he had to offer God was a broken spirit and a broken and contrite heart.

4. Praying for God's blessing (vv. 18–19). The psalmist prayed for God's blessing toward Jerusalem (v. 18). He said that God would be pleased with sacrifices when they signified a repentant heart and a righteous life (v. 19).

APPLYING THE BIBLE

1. **"Sin had made me crazy."** In one of his hymns, Reformer Martin Luther writes:

> *In devil's dungeon chained I lay*
> *the pangs of death swept o'er me.*
> *My sin devoured me night and day*
> *In which my mother bore me.*
> *My anguish grew more rife,*
> *I took no pleasure in my life*
> *And sin had made me crazy.*

An Old Testament scholar, the late Kyle Yates, says this psalm we are studying is David's confession of sin with Bathsheba (2 Sam. 11). Yates writes: "For almost a year David endured the lashing of an active conscience. . . . One day Nathan (the prophet) came with the powerful thrust that left the king conscious of his sin and able to sense something of his tragic condition before a just and holy God. His heart was crushed. . . . [and] he readily admitted: 'I have sinned against God.'" [1]

Like Luther, David's sin had almost driven him crazy, but turning to God in repentance, he found God's forgiveness and cleansing (vv. 1–12).

2. **The wideness of God's mercy.** Frederick W. Faber (1814–1863) was an Anglican clergyman who, in 1846, became a Roman Catholic. After embracing Catholicism, Faber composed many hymns, one hundred and fifty of which are still sung in worship services today. Some are not too well known, but among his most popular hymns are "Faith of Our Fathers" and "There's a Wideness in God's Mercy." Often we have sung both of them, never knowing they were written by a pious Roman Catholic. The latter hymn reads:

> *There's a wideness in God's mercy,*
> *Like the wideness of the sea;*
> *There's a kindness in His justice,*
> *Which is more than liberty.*
> *There is welcome for the sinner,*
> *And graces from the good;*
> *There is mercy with the Savior;*
> *There is healing in His blood.* [2]

With his sin crushing the life and vitality out of him, what was David's greatest need? It was for the mercy of God to cover Him and the grace of God to cleanse him (vv. 1–2). And that is our greatest need, too.

3. Can you relate to David's plea for forgiveness and cleansing? If you can't, your heart is harder than you think. To be led and filled with the Holy Spirit means to be sensitive to sin, sorrowful over it, and to seek cleansing in the blood of Jesus. That is just as true for "respectable sins," such as withholding our tithes from God, as it is for heinous sins such as adultery.

I remember as a child doing a bad thing that was contrary to being a Christian (not the one to which I referred in an earlier lesson). Guilt poured over me and made me feel terrible. But I closed my heart and refused to deal with it in repentance. For months I refused to seek God's forgiveness, but then the day came when I could no longer stand the weight of guilt and made a clean breast of it all. Then the peace of God flooded my heart like a mighty ocean of forgiveness. I learned an invaluable lesson as a child that has served me well, as David learned the same lesson as a king: the only answer to sin and guilt is confession and forgiveness (vv. 2–10).

4. God is present. Carolus Linnaeus (1707–1778) was a renowned authority on plants who developed the modern, scientific method of naming plants and animals. Given $50 by the Royal Society of Science, he spent five months in 1732 collecting plants in Lapland, traveling 4,800 miles and walking nearly 1,000 miles.

Over the entrance to his laboratory, Linnaeus had carved his motto. Translated from Latin, it read: "Do not sully hand and heart today. Deity is present." When the king's lust for Bathsheba was so fierce it led to adultery and murder, the memory that God is always present with us would have saved him a world of grief (v. 11). And when we are tempted to sin, let us, too, remember that God is a witness to our every word, thought, and deed.

TEACHING THE BIBLE

▶ *Main Idea:* David's prayer of confession and repentance demonstrates that we must confess and repent of our sin.
▶ *Suggested Teaching Aim:* To lead adults to examine David's prayer of confession and repentance, and to determine how God wants them to respond to Him

A TEACHING OUTLINE

1. Use an illustration to introduce the session.
2. Use a lesson poster to guide the Bible study.
3. Use a creative writing assignment to apply the Scripture.

Introduce the Bible Study
Use "Sin had made me crazy" from "Applying the Bible" to introduce the session.
Search for Biblical Truth
IN ADVANCE, make a lesson poster with the following headings. Leave space for writing four points under the first heading and two

points under the second heading.

Repent and Confess
I. Praying to God for Forgiveness (Ps. 51:1–12)
II. Offering a Changed Life (Ps. 51:13–19)

Place this poster on the focal wall for all to see.

Call attention to the first point on the poster. Ask members to open their Bibles to Psalm 51:1–2. Ask: In these two verses, what words did David use to describe God? (Mercy, lovingkindness, and tender mercies.) Use the information in "Studying the Bible" to explain the significance of each of these words.

Ask: What three words did David use in 51:1–2 to describe his sins? (Transgressions, iniquity, sin.) Use the information in "Studying the Bible" to explain the variation of meaning in these three words. Ask: What three words or phrases did David use to describe the forgiveness he sought? (Sins blotted out, washed, cleansed.)

Point out that David described at least four steps that he went through to pray for forgiveness. Write the following phrases on the lesson poster under the first heading and ask members to suggest which verses would support these statements. The suggested answers are in parentheses.

1. Praying to the merciful God (51–12)
2. Confessing sins (51:3–6)
3. Seeking cleansing (51:7–9)
4. Asking for renewal (51:10–12)

DISCUSS: How could David say his sin was against God when he committed adultery with Bathsheba? How does God create a clean heart in us? What do you need to do to have the joy of your salvation restored?

Point out the second statement on the lesson poster. Ask members to read silently 51:13,17. Write the following phrases on the chalkboard or a large sheet of paper and ask members to suggest which verses would support these statements. The suggested answers are in parentheses.

1. Converting sinners (51:13)
2. Offering oneself (51:17)

Ask: In addition to these two evidences of forgiveness, what other evidences would you suggest? Add them to your list.

DISCUSS: If we do not want to share our faith with others, is our faith genuine? If we do not tell others who have fallen into sin that they can find forgiveness, who will? What kind of sacrifices does God want you to offer?

Give the Truth a Personal Focus
Call attention to the two points on the lesson poster. Ask: Which area—seeking forgiveness or showing you have been forgiven—is the greatest need of your life? Ask members to determine how God wants them to respond to Him. Distribute paper and pencils. Ask members to write a psalm of their own in which they ask God for forgiveness that incorporates the elements of this psalm. Ask for volunteers to read theirs to the class but do not force anyone.

---

1. Kyle Yates, *Preaching from the Psalms* (Nashville: Broadman Press, 1948), 3.

2. *Broadman Hymnal* (Nashville: Convention Press, 1975 edition), 171.

Worship and Witness

Basic Passage: Psalm 96
Focal Passage: Psalm 96

P salm 96 is preserved in slightly different words in 1 Chronicles 16:23–33. Psalm 96, along with Psalm 105:1–15 and parts of other psalms, was sung when the ark of the covenant was brought to Jerusalem. Psalm 96 is an invitation for all people and all creation to join in praise to God as Creator, King, and Judge.

▶ ▶ ▶ ▶ ▶ ▶ ▶ ▶ **Study Aim:** *To explain why worship and witness are insep-arable*

STUDYING THE BIBLE

LESSON OUTLINE
I. Sing Unto the Lord, All the Earth (Ps. 96:1–6)
  1. Call to sing praises to the Lord (Ps. 96:1–3)
  2. The greatness of the Lord (Ps. 96:4–6)
II. Call to Worship the Lord as King (Ps. 96:7–13)
  1. Give God the glory due His name (Ps. 96:7–9)
  2. God as King and Judge (Ps. 96:10–13)

The psalmist invited all the earth to join in singing unto the Lord and called people of faith to bear witness to Him (vv. 1–3). The psalmist proclaimed the greatness of the Creator over all idols (vv. 4–6). He called all people to give the Lord the glory due His name (vv. 7–9). He called on all people and things to recognize God as reigning and coming King and Judge (vv. 10–13).

I. Sing unto the Lord, All the Earth (Ps. 96:1–6)

1. Call to sing praises to the Lord (vv. 1–3)

1 O sing unto the Lord a new song: sing unto the Lord, all the earth.

2 Sing unto the Lord, bless his name; shew forth his salvation from day to day.

3 Declare his glory among the heathen, his wonders among all people.

Verses 1–3 show several aspects of true worship. One is that worship includes singing. The word *sing* is found throughout the Book of Psalms because these were hymns designed to be sung. Throughout history, singing has been an essential part of worship. Singing, with its melody and poetic wording, is ideal for expressing the feelings of true worship. Such singing is not just sung to and for one another, but "unto the Lord." Singing in worship is praise directed to the Lord Himself.

Another aspect of true worship is that it is inseparable from witness. The word translated "shew forth" in verse 2 literally means "to tell good tidings." The worshipers were called to bless the name of the Lord and to tell the good news of His salvation. Verse 3 uses the word "declare" to make the same point. Witness is part of worship, and worship leads to witness in daily life. After Isaiah had a tremendous experience of worship, he heard the call of God and volunteered to bear God's message (see Isa. 6:1–8). Worship without witness would fall short of true worship. Witness with worship would be shallow and lifeless.

The recipients of the witness were not only the people of God but also all people. The call to sing unto the Lord was issued to "all the earth." The worshipers were to declare God's glory "among the heathen" and to tell of His mighty works "among all people." During this year, we have studied Old Testament passages that stressed the universal nature of Israel's faith. Among these were the final chapters of Isaiah, the Book of Jonah, and the Book of Ruth. This theme appears not only in verses 1 and 3 of Psalm 96, but also in many of the other verses.

Another aspect of true worship is that it must be renewed. The "new song" of verse 1 is mentioned in other psalms (see 33:3; 40:3; 98:1; 149:1). At some point, of course, each of these was a new song in the sense of having been newly composed. However, each of them continued to be a new song in the sense of expressing the renewal of worship. Just as God's mercies are new every day (Lam. 3:22–23), so singing His praises should be new every day. Notice also the words "from day to day" in verse 2. Both worship and witness should be part of our daily living.

2. The greatness of the Lord (vv. 4–6)

4 For the Lord is great, and greatly to be praised: he is to be feared above all gods.

Many people claim to believe in God, but they do not respond to God the way the Bible says that people respond to the true and living God. They believe in an impersonal god, an abstract god, not in the great and good Lord. One of the acid tests of true faith is whether one's professed faith results in praise to God. Some people use the right words to describe the god in whom they believe. Many would affirm with the psalmist that the Lord is great; however, their actions show they don't respond by praising Him greatly.

5 For all the gods of the nations are idols: but the Lord made the heavens.

Idolatry was widely practiced in ancient times, as indeed it still is, although often in different forms than the images of ancient people. The Old Testament contains some scathing denunciations of idolatry. Isaiah 44, for example, describes how images of gods were created by human hands. People took a piece of wood. With part of it they built various items for their own use. Part of it was burned to make a fire on which they cooked. Part of it was shaped into an image before which they bowed in worship (see vv. 9–20).

Over against idols, created by men, the psalmist set the only true and living God, who is the Creator of all things. God created the heavens and the earth and all that is in them. What folly to put our trust and give our allegiance to other objects of worship, which are our own creations, subject to the failings of their human creators and totally unable to help us in our needs.

> **6 Honour and majesty are before him: strength and beauty are in his sanctuary.**

The psalmist sought words that were worthy of describing this great God, who created all things and whom we worship. He used "honour and majesty," which were words used to describe the royal dignity of earthly kings. The psalmist used these words of the King over all things and all people.

He also used "strength and beauty" to describe God in His sanctuary. An increasing number of people profess to believe that public worship is unimportant in their lives. Some of these are people who claim to be able to worship God just as well in nature as with the congregation in the house of the Lord. I often wonder if such excuse-makers worship God anywhere. People of faith worship God in nature, in the quietness of their place of prayer, and within the congregation of other people of faith.

II. Call to Worship the Lord as King (Ps. 96:7–13)

1. Give God the glory due His name (vv. 7–9)

> **7 Give unto the Lord, O ye kindreds of the people, give unto the Lord glory and strength.**
>
> **8 Give unto the Lord the glory due unto his name: bring an offering, and come into his courts.**

Verses 7–9 continue the call for all people to worship the Lord. "Kindreds of the people" can be translated "families of nations" (NIV). The call is to "all the earth."

The word *glory* is a key word in the Bible. The basic meaning of the Hebrew word is heavy in weight. The verb came to be used of giving weight or honor to something. To glorify God is to recognize the essential being of God that gives Him importance and weight in relationship with the people who are worshiping Him. To put it another way, to give glory to God means to give Him the kind of honor that matches His true weight or character.

God's reputation is often far short of His true character. People do not see God as He truly is; as a result, they don't give Him the love, honor, and obedience He deserves. This is what the psalmist meant by giving God "the glory due unto his name." God's name is the character of God as He truly is, not as sinful, unbelieving people think He is. The purpose of worship and witness is to give God the glory due His name.

The last part of verse 8 mentions another aspect of worship. People show their faith and love by bringing offerings to God as part of their worship. In our study of the psalms, we have noted that God doesn't want offerings that are made as substitutes for repentance and obedience (see Pss. 51:16–17; 40:6–8). On the other hand, when we have first of all offered ourselves to the Lord, offerings are expressions of our faith and love to the Lord. In Christian churches, offerings also support witness to the people of the world who are called to know and glorify God.

9 O worship the Lord in the beauty of holiness: fear before him, all the earth.

Worship involves coming into the presence of the holy God. Although through Christ we are encouraged to come boldly to the throne of grace (Heb. 4:16), we are also told to come with a sense of reverence and awe.

2. God as King and Judge (vv. 10–13)

10 Say among the heathen that the Lord reigneth: the world also shall be established that it shall not be moved: he shall judge the people righteously.

11 Let the heavens rejoice, and let the earth be glad; let the sea roar, and the fulness thereof.

12 Let the field be joyful, and all that is therein: then shall all the trees of the wood rejoice

13 Before the Lord: for he cometh, for he cometh to judge the earth: he shall judge the world with righteousness, and the people with his truth.

Verse 10 contains the clearest statement of the call to witness to all people. God's people were to declare to the heathen that the Lord reigns. In other words, the people of Israel were called to declare that their God was King and Judge over all the earth, not just over their people and land. Such Old Testament passages foreshadowed the time in God's plan when Spirit-led followers of Jesus Christ would receive the Great Commission (see Matt. 28:18–20; see also Acts 1:8). The people of Israel were chosen not just for their own blessings but in order to be channels of blessings to all nations (see Gen. 12:1–3).

Psalm 96 proclaims the reality of God as reigning King and functioning Judge over all the earth; however, verse 13 recognized that the full revelation of His rule and judgment lay in the future. When Jesus came, He came declaring that the kingdom or reign of God had come (see Mark 1:15); yet He also taught His followers to pray, "Thy kingdom come" (Matt. 6:10). Even we who live in light of God's new covenant are still living in a world that doesn't recognize the eternal King and Judge. Only people of faith dare to believe that God's righteousness and truth will have the final word. The world in which we live is much like the world of the psalmist. Injustice and evil often seem to be the only realities. We need to heed the words of verses 10 and 13. We must tell the world that the Lord already reigns and they can acknowledge Him by faith. We also need to share the word that His kingdom will come. This is a word of judgment to some and a word of encouragement to others.

Verses 11–12 are a call to all God's creation to join in praising Him. These verses show that all the earth means more than all the people of the earth. These verses call all of nature to praise God. The sea is to praise Him with its roar. The fields and everything in them are to be jubilant. The trees are called to sing for joy.

1. Ira Sankey's life saved by singing. America's best-known preacher during the last century was evangelist Dwight L. Moody. And Moody's singer who sang to the thousands who attended Moody's services was Ira D. Sankey.

One Christmas Eve, Sankey was asked to sing as he traveled up the Delaware River. After the song had ended, a man came up to Sankey and asked him if he had served in the Union Army, and if he were standing guard on a clear, moonlight night in the spring of 1861. When Sankey said he had, the man, a Confederate veteran, told Sankey: "I had you in my sights and was about to pull the trigger when you began to sing the hymn: 'We are thine, do thou befriend us,/Be the guardian of our way.' I waited for you to finish singing, saying to myself, 'I'll kill him when he finishes.' But the hymn brought back memories of my mother singing it to me as a child long ago, and I couldn't pull the trigger."

Knowing the power of singing hymns to lift the spirit and to praise God, the psalmist encourages us to sing (vv. 1–3).

2. Bearing witness to Jesus. In one of his books Paul Powell, president of the Southern Baptist Annuity Board, tells about a sign he saw in a Colorado motel: "There ain't hardly no business here that ain't been gone after!"

God is not only concerned about what we believe, but also about the faithfulness with which we serve. A Quaker service was just breaking up when a late member rushed up, asking, "Is the service over?" "Yes," said a friend, "the meeting is over, but the service has only begun!"

He hit the nail right on the head! We worship to replenish our spiritual strength in order to serve God in our communities. Worship is to be followed by witnessing, as the psalmist practiced in his day (vv. 1–11). We must remember in witnessing to the unsaved, "there ain't hardly no business here that ain't been gone after." We are to go after them and bring them in (vv. 3–10).

3. Who or what is your God? Each of us worships a god of some kind. Perhaps it is the God of creation who has fully revealed Himself in Jesus Christ. Perhaps not. The priority in our life is our god. To what do you give the most attention? On what do you spend your money? What most occupies your mind and thoughts? Perhaps it is family, or your business, or your savings accounts, or your stocks and bonds. Each of us must search our heart and let God speak to us and show us if we have any other gods before Him (Exod. 20:3). There is no rest for the soul until it forsakes all man-made gods and bows before the true God in repentance and faith. Well did Augustine, the fourth-century church father, put it when he said: "My soul is restless until it can rest in Thee, O God."

This is what the psalmist of our lesson says to us today in verses 4–6.

4. Giving glory to God. With a good concordance, check to see how many times the word *glory* appears in the Bible. You will be amazed.

Above all things, God wants to be glorified in His people and in His creation. And more is said about the glory of God in the Book of Psalms than in any other book of the Bible. The word in the Old Testament refers to "the weighty importance and shining majesty which accompany God's presence. . . . The New Testament uses 'doxa' [doxology] to express glory and limits the meaning to God's glory. . . . [and the] New Testament carries forth the Old Testament meaning of divine power and majesty. The New Testament extends this to Christ as having divine glory (Luke 9:32; John 1:14; 1 Cor. 2:8)."[1]

5. The King is coming. When I was a boy, I remember how I felt in turning the last corner in the road that led home from school. The days often were very cold and, most of the winter, snow lay on the ground. I would often see in the near distance my mother's face framed by the kitchen window, and I knew the house was warm and smelled of good things such as sugar cookies.

Why did my mother keep her daily vigil so faithfully? It was because she knew her son was coming home and she wanted to see him, hug him, and welcome him home.

With that same kind of joy and anticipation, we who are followers of Christ must expect His coming and be ready when He comes for us (vv. 10–13).

TEACHING THE BIBLE

▶ *Main Idea:* The relationship of worship and witness point out that the two are inseparable.
▶ *Suggested Teaching Aim:* To lead adults to examine the relationship between worship and witness, and to identify ways their worship can be a witness.

A TEACHING OUTLINE

1. Use an illustration to begin the session.
2. Use a research project to involve a member.
3. Use Scripture search to identify elements of true worship.
4. Use a group project to identify how your worship services can be a witness to nonbelievers.

Introduce the Bible Study
Use "Ira Sankey's life saved by singing" from "Applying the Bible" to begin the session. Point out that our psalm today—Psalm 96—encourages singing to the Lord.

Search for Biblical Truth
IN ADVANCE, enlist a member to read "Hymn" in the *Holman Bible Dictionary* or another dictionary and report on how singing was used in the Old Testament.

On a chalkboard or a large sheet of paper write, True Worship. Ask: What elements should be present in true worship? Ask members to open their Bibles to Psalm 96 and call for a volunteer to read these verses. Ask members to provide answers from these verses. Be sure the following elements are listed. Share the suggested information and use the discussion questions.

Singing (vv. 1–2). (1) Psalms were designed to be sung; (2) Singing should be "unto the Lord" and is praise directed to the Lord Himself. Call for the report on "Hymns" in the Old Testament at this point.

DISCUSS: What is the purpose of singing? Is it to make us feel good or to honor God? Why? How can we know the difference? When is singing not "unto the Lord"?

Witness (vv. 2,10–13). Witness is part of worship, and worship should lead to witness in daily life.

DISCUSS: Are we engaging in true worship if our worship does not lead us to witness to the whole world?

Renewed (v. 3). Worship should be new and fresh; we should be willing to sing "new songs."

DISCUSS: How can we balance remembering God's mighty acts of deliverance (Ps. 105:5) and singing a new song?

Praising and magnifying God (vv. 4–6). Our actions in magnifying God must back up our words. God alone has "honor and majesty" and "strength and beauty."

DISCUSS: What false gods can we honor in our worship services? What elements of our worship do not praise God?

Offering (v. 8). God doesn't want offerings as a substitute for repentance and obedience; He wants them as an expression of our faith and love.

DISCUSS: What purposes does bringing an offering serve in our worship today?

Accountability (v. 13). God will have the final word. This will be a word of judgment to some and a word of encouragement to others.

DISCUSS: Why would you fear or welcome God's judgment? After you have listed all of the elements of worship members can find in these verses, ask: Do all worship experiences have to have these elements in them? Which ones could be left out and still be true worship?

Give the Truth a Personal Focus

Use a church bulletin and ask members to examine the elements of worship. Which parts of the service are designed for members only? Which parts would appeal to nonbelievers? Which parts would make nonbelievers feel uncomfortable?

Ask members to list ways your worship services could be a witness. Suggest they approach this question by pretending they are complete pagans and have never been in a Christian worship service before. What would make them feel uncomfortable? at home? welcomed?

Share your list with those who plan your worship.

---

1. *Holman's Bible Dictionary* (Nashville: Holman Bible Publishers, 1991), 557.)

Holding Fast to the Lord

Background Passage: 2 Kings 18–20
Focal Passages: 2 Kings 18:1–8; 20:16–21

T he reign of Hezekiah (hez ih KIGH uh) is treated at great length because he was a good king who trusted in the Lord and also because of his association with Isaiah. (Most of 2 Kings 18–20 is also found in Isaiah 37–39.) Generally speaking, Hezekiah and Isaiah shared the same spirit of trust in the Lord. On a few occasions, Isaiah was forced to condemn Hezekiah; however, these were the exception rather than the rule. The emphasis in the Bible passage is on Hezekiah's trust in holding fast to the Lord.

▶ ▶ ▶ ▶ **Study Aim:** *To identify evidences of Hezekiah's trust in holding fast to the Lord.*

STUDYING THE BIBLE

Outline and Summary
I. Hezekiah and His Reforms (2 Kings 18:1–8)
1. Good King Hezekiah (18:1–3)
2. Hezekiah's reforms (18:4)
3. Hezekiah's trust in the Lord (18:5–8)
II. The Assyrian Threat (2 Kings 18:9–37)
1. The fall of Israel (18:9–12)
2. Tribute to Assyria (18:13–16)
3. Jerusalem threatened (18:17–37)
III.Jerusalem Delivered (2 Kings 19:1–37)
1. Isaiah's reassurance to Hezekiah (19:1–7)
2. Hezekiah's prayer (19:8–19)
3. Isaiah's prophecy and its fulfillment (19:20–37)
IV. Hezekiah's Illness and Healing (2 Kings 20:1–11)
V. Hezekiah and the Envoys from Babylon (2 Kings 20:12–19)
1. Revealing Judah's treasures (20:12–15)
2. Prophecy of captivity in Babylon (20:16–18)
3. Hezekiah's response (20:19)
VI. Hezekiah's Achievements (2 Kings 20:20–21)

Hezekiah was a good king (18:1–3) who sought to destroy idolatry (18:4). His steadfast trust in the Lord resulted in the Lord's blessings (18:5–8). During Hezekiah's reign, the Assyrians (uh SIRH ih uns) defeated the Northern Kingdom (18:9–12). When the Assyrians captured some cities in Judah, Hezekiah paid tribute to them (18:13–16). The Assyrian army threatened to capture Jerusalem (18:17–37). When Hezekiah appealed to Isaiah, the prophet reassured him (19:1–7). After the Assyrians continued to send their threats, Hezekiah prayed for deliverance (19:8–19). Isaiah's prophecy of deliverance came to pass (19:20–27). When Hezekiah was deathly ill, God responded to his prayers by lengthening his life (20:1–11). After Hezekiah showed Judah's treasures to envoys from Babylon (BAB ih lahn; 20:12–15), Isaiah predicted Judah's Babylonian captivity (20:16–18). Hezekiah declared that God's ways are good (20:19). Among Hezekiah's accomplishments was a water system for Jerusalem (20:20–21).

I. Hezekiah and His Reforms (2 Kings 18:1–8)

1. Good King Hezekiah (18:1–3)

1 Now it came to pass in the third year of Hoshea [hoh SHE uh] son of Elah [EE luh] king of Israel, that Hezekiah the son of Ahaz [AY haz] king of Judah began to reign.

2 Twenty and five years old was he when he began to reign; and he reigned twenty and nine years in Jerusalem. His mother's name also was Abi [AY bigh], the daughter of Zachariah [zak uh RIGH uh].

3 And he did that which was right in the sight of the Lord, according to all that David his father did.

Hezekiah began to reign over Judah during the final years of their sister kingdom to the north (2 Kings 17). The most notable fact about Hezekiah was that he did what was right in the sight of the Lord. This was in striking contrast to most of Judah's kings. For example, Ahaz, Hezekiah's father "did not *that which was* right in the sight of the LORD his God" (2 Kings 16:2).

How do we explain an evil father having a good son? Perhaps Hezekiah had a godly mother. All we know of her is her name, but she may have been a person of faith. Isaiah had begun his ministry as Ahaz began his sixteen–year reign (Isa. 1:1; 6:1; 2 Kings 16:2). Thus Isaiah was around when Hezekiah was growing up.

Everyone is exposed to good and bad influences, and each person decides which influence to follow. Hezekiah decided not to follow the example of his father but to listen to people like Isaiah. Sadly, Hezekiah's own son Manasseh (muh NASS uh) rejected the example of his father and the words of Isaiah (2 Kings 21:1–18).

2. Hezekiah's reforms (18:4)

4 He removed the high places, and brake the images, and cut down the groves, and brake in pieces the brasen serpent that Moses had made: for unto those days the children of Israel did burn incense to it: and he called it Nehushtan [nih HUHSH tan].

Judah had adopted the practices of pagan people. "High places" were Canaanite (KAY nuhn ight) shrines to Baal (BAY uhl; 2 Kings 16:4). The word *groves* is literally "Asherah" (ASH uh ruh), the female consort of Baal. This shows that Hezekiah attacked the remnants of Baal worship. He also set out to destroy other expressions of pagan worship.

Verse 4 reveals a striking example of the people's bent toward idolatry. They were even worshiping the brazen serpent that the Lord had used in the wilderness as a sign of divine deliverance (see Num. 21:4–9; John 3:14–15).

3. Hezekiah's trust in the Lord (18:5–8)

5 He trusted in the Lord God of Israel; so that after him was none like him among all the kings of Judah, nor any that were before him.

6 For he clave to the Lord, and departed not from following him, but kept his commandments, which the Lord commanded Moses.

7 And the Lord was with him; and he prospered whithersoever he went forth: and he rebelled against the king of Assyria, and served him not.

8 He smote the Philistines [fih LISS teens], even unto Gaza [GAY zuh], and the borders thereof, from the tower of the watchmen to the fenced city.

Verse 5 uses the usual Hebrew word for "trust" to describe Hezekiah's uncommon reliance on God. At least, such trust was uncommon among the kings of Judah. The word *clave* in verse 6 is the same word used in Genesis 2:24 for the oneness of a husband and wife. Hezekiah held fast to the Lord and joined himself together with the Lord. Verse 6 also stresses that Hezekiah's trust in God was expressed in obedience to the commands of God.

Verse 7 adds that "the LORD was with him." This closeness was the result of trusting in, cleaving to, and obeying the Lord. The evidence of the Lord's abiding presence was the success of Hezekiah in achieving his objectives. Specifically, the king of tiny Judah found the courage to stand against the power of the mighty Assyrian king. Hezekiah's armies also prevailed in battles with their longtime enemies, the Philistines.

II. The Assyrian Threat (2 Kings 18:9–37)

1. **The fall of Israel (18:9–12).** During Hezekiah's reign, the Northern Kingdom was overrun by the Assyrians. The survivors were carried away and transplanted in other lands (see 2 Kings 17).

2. **Tribute to Assyria (18:13–16).** After destroying Israel, the Assyrians swarmed into Judah. After the Assyrians captured outlying cities, Hezekiah sent gold and silver as tribute to the Assyrian king.

3. **Jerusalem threatened (18:17–37).** The king of Assyria sent messengers to insist that Hezekiah surrender. The messengers warned against relying on Egypt for help. The messengers spoke loudly enough to be heard by defenders on the walls of Jerusalem. The Assyrians warned the Judeans that they would suffer and die if they allowed their king and their God to deceive them into resisting the might of Assyria.

III. Jerusalem Delivered (2 Kings 19:1–37)

1. **Isaiah's reassurance to Hezekiah (19:1–7).** Hezekiah sent messengers to Isaiah. The prophet told Hezekiah's officials not to be afraid of the Assyrians because God would send them back to their country.

2. Hezekiah's prayer (19:8–19). After the Assyrians sent another threatening message, the Judean king spread it before the Lord and prayed for deliverance.

3. Isaiah's prophecy and its fulfillment (19:20–37). The Lord's response was to send a message through Isaiah to Hezekiah. God was in control of events, including the boastful Assyrians. God promised that the land that was now threatened with war and famine would bloom and bear fruit. As for the king of Assyria, he would not shoot an arrow against the city that God defended. Thousands of the Assyrians died in their camp, and the king returned home, where he was assassinated.

IV. Hezekiah's Illness and Healing
(2 Kings 20:1–11)

When Hezekiah became ill, Isaiah told him that he would die. Hezekiah prayed earnestly that he might live. Isaiah returned to assure the king that God had added fifteen years to his life.

V. Hezekiah and the Envoys from Babylon
(2 Kings 20:12–19)

1. Revealing Judah's treasures (20:12–15). When envoys from Babylon arrived in Jerusalem, Hezekiah welcomed them and showed them Judah's storehouses of treasures. When Isaiah quizzed Hezekiah about the visitors and Hezekiah's actions, the king related what he had done.

2. Prophecy of captivity in Babylon (20:16–18)

16 And Isaiah said unto Hezekiah, Hear the word of the Lord.

17 Behold, the days come, that all that is in thine house, and that which thy fathers have laid up in store unto this day, shall be carried into Babylon: nothing shall be left, saith the Lord.

18 And of thy sons that shall issue from thee, which thou shalt beget, shall they take away; and they shall be eunuchs in the palace of the king of Babylon.

After Hezekiah had shown the treasures to the Babylonians, Isaiah predicted that the time would come when Babylonians would seize all Judah's treasures. Isaiah also predicted that Hezekiah's royal descendants would be taken to Babylon and become eunuchs in the palace of the king of Babylon. The Hebrew word *eunuch* sometimes referred to a literal eunuch; at other times, the word was used of a government official (Gen. 37:36; 39:1).

Assyria was the dominant power in the time of Hezekiah and Isaiah. Isaiah, however, warned that when Babylon became the dominant power, the Babylonians would defeat Judah. Many years after the time of Isaiah. Babylon defeated Judah and carried her king and treasures away (2 Kings 24:8–16).

3. Hezekiah's response (20:19)

19 Then said Hezekiah unto Isaiah, Good is the word of the Lord which thou hast spoken. And he said, Is it not good, if peace and truth be in my days?

There are two ways of understanding Hezekiah's words. According to the first view, he was unconcerned about what later generations would endure—as long as he personally would not have to endure it. According to the second view, verse 19 expresses trust that God's ways have a good purpose and gratitude that Hezekiah's own generation would know peace and security.

VI. Hezekiah's Achievements
(2 Kings 20:20-21)

20 And the rest of the acts of Hezekiah, and all his might, and how he made a pool, and a conduit, and brought water into the city, are they not written in the book of the chronicles of the kings of Judah?

21 And Hezekiah slept with his fathers: and Manasseh his son reigned in his stead.

Among Hezekiah's other achievements was the construction of a water system for Jerusalem. This and other deeds of Hezekiah are recorded in 2 Chronicles 29-32.

APPLYING THE BIBLE

1. Trust anyone under thirty? Several years ago, an internationally read magazine printed an article asking the question, "Can you trust everyone under thirty?" The article set me to thinking: John Keats wrote "Ode to a Grecian Urn" and "Endymion" before he died at 26. William Cullen Bryant, the father of American poetry, wrote "Thanatopsis" when he was about twenty. Thomas Jefferson was less than thirty when the Senate had to suspend its rules so he could be seated and was only thirty-four when he wrote the "Declaration of Independence."

Patriot Nathan Hale was only twenty-one when he cried, "All I regret is that I have but one life to give for my country." The Pilgrim fathers averaged only twenty-six years of age. Joan of Arc led France to victory when she was just sixteen. Johannes Brahms was only twenty when he composed piano pieces that are still being played today.

Hezekiah was only twenty-five when he ascended the throne of Judah, "and he did that which was right in the sight of the Lord" (v. 3).

2. In spite of. Many people have accomplished much in spite of difficulties. In spite of having only a year of formal schooling, Abraham Lincoln became president of the United States and freed four million black slaves with his Emancipation Proclamation. In spite of suffering twelve years in Bedford, England's jail, John Bunyan used his time well in writing The Pilgrim's Progress. In spite of a drunken father and deafness that set in at twenty-eight, so that by fifty-nine he could communicate only by writing, Beethoven composed deathless masterpieces. In spite of having only three months of formal education and near deafness, Thomas A. Edison patented more inventions than any other person in history.

And in spite of idolatry and turmoil within Judah and crises outside of Judah, Hezekiah stood by his convictions "and clave to the

Lord, and departed not from following him" (18:6). He is a good example of one who served God faithfully and is listed in the genealogy of Jesus (Matt. 1:9–10 as "Ezekias"). He left a good example for us to emulate.

3. Touching others.

My life shall touch a dozen lives
Before the day is done;
Leave countless marks for good or ill,
Ere sets the evening sun.
So this the wish I always wish,
the prayer I ever pray;
Lord, may my life help other lives
It touches by the way.

—Anonymous

4. We are witnesses for good or evil. We probably don't understand the scope of our influence as Christians for good or evil. People are watching us and listening to us all the time. And our behavior points them to Christ or away from them.

An incident in the life of the late President Theodore Roosevelt illustrates this. On an extended vacation one summer, Roosevelt met an unusual man everyone called "Uncle Joe." As Roosevelt was leaving after a pleasant hour of visiting with Uncle Joe, the old man said, "Mr. President, we have a lovely little church here in our village, but I haven't seen you in our services any Sunday you have been here. I know you are a Christian gentleman, and your coming would mean so much to our people."

Roosevelt said he felt thoroughly chastised and humbled and promised he would be there the following Sunday, and he never missed another Sunday service when he was there on vacation. Later, Roosevelt confessed he was ashamed of himself before his Heavenly Father for being such a poor witness for Him.

Hezekiah ruled Judah for twenty-five years and, although he was far from perfect, he strove to serve God faithfully and honor Him daily (vv. 5–7).

5. A man sent from God. John Wesley, the founder of Methodism, once preached the gospel among the miners of Cornwall, England. Many people and villages were transformed.

A stranger visiting the Cornwall district once asked about the picture of Wesley he saw hanging in so many homes, and he was told: "There was a man sent from God whose name was John."

Hezekiah was a man sent from God who made a mighty impact on Judah and her surrounding neighbors in a most critical period of Judah's history. And God used Hezekiah mightily. In doing God's will faithfully we, too, will make a contribution to the lives of others that will live on long after we are gone.

TEACHING THE BIBLE

▶ *Main Idea:* God supports those who trust Him and hold fast to Him.
▶ *Suggested Teaching Aim:* To encourage adults to trust God and to hold fast to Him

A TEACHING OUTLINE

1. Introduce the Bible study by sharing an illustration.
2. Enlist members to help you in summarizing and presenting the material.
3. Use lecture and group discussion to search for biblical truth.
4. Use brainstorming to help members apply the Scripture to their lives.

Introduce the Bible Study

Use the illustration, "In spite of" from "Applying the Bible" to introduce the Bible study.

Search for Biblical Truth

IN ADVANCE, prepare a lesson outline poster like the one on page 57 and display it on the focal wall. Also enlist one or more members to summarize the following segments: 2 Kings 18:9–37; 2 Kings 19:1–37; and 2 Kings 20:1–11. Give the member(s) the material from "Studying the Bible." Call on them at the appropriate time.

Since the background passage covers so much material, enlist two readers to read alternately the eleven statements of the summary to introduce the lesson at this point.

Call for a volunteer to read 2 Kings 18:13. Using Holman Bible Dictionary or another Bible dictionary, give a brief summary of Hezekiah's life. Point out that Hezekiah and Isaiah lived at approximately the same time.

Ask a volunteer to read 18:4 and let members list Hezekiah's reforms. Explain "high places," "images," "groves," and "brasen serpent." (See "Studying the Bible" for help.)

Ask a volunteer to read 18:5–8. Ask: What successes did Hezekiah have? (Prospered, rebelled against Assyria, defeated Philistines.) What in these verses indicates why he could do this? (He trusted, clave to, departed not from, kept commandments of, the Lord.)

DISCUSS: What would you have to do to trust, cleave to, depart not from, and keep the commandments of the Lord? How would this change the way you live? Would the United States experience the same benefits Israel did if their leaders responded to the Lord the same as Hezekiah? Why?

Call on the enlisted member(s) to summarize 2 Kings 18:9–20:15.

Ask a volunteer to read 20:16–18. Set the context for these verses by explaining Hezekiah's foolish response to the Babylonians. Point out the approximate date of Hezekiah's reign (716–687 B.C) and that although Jerusalem did not fall until a hundred years after his death, Isaiah's prophecy was fulfilled.

Call for a volunteer to read 20:19. Ask members what they think Hezekiah's response meant. Use "Studying the Bible" to explain two possible meanings.

Call for a volunteer to read 20:20–21. If you have access to the

Holman Bible Dictionary, show the photograph of the tunnel Hezekiah constructed to bring water into the city from the Gihon (GIGH hahn) Spring outside the city. Point out that the reference to the "book of the chronicles of the kings of Judah" is our 2 Chronicles 29–32.

Give the Truth a Personal Focus

Ask: Do you believe that God still blesses those who trust in Him? How? Why?

Ask members to suggest steps they can take to increase their trust in the Lord. List these on a chalkboard or a large sheet of paper.

Suggest members select one of these ways and commit themselves to trust God in this area. Close in a prayer of commitment.

Obeying God's Commands

Basic Passage: 2 Kings 22:1–23:20
Focal Passage: 2 Kings 23:1–8a

H ezekiah (hez ih KIGH uh) and Josiah (joh SIGH uh) were Judah's two best kings. Hezekiah is remembered for holding fast to the Lord when Assyria threatened to overrun Judah. Josiah is remembered for a religious revival inspired by a new awareness of God's Word. Two wicked kings—Manasseh (muh NASS uh) and Amon (AY mahn)—reigned between Hezekiah and Josiah (see 2 Kings 21). Their evil policies had polluted the temple and almost destroyed the worship of the Lord. Josiah tried to undo their evil and to restore Judah to obedience to God's commands.

▶ ▶ ▶ ▶ **Study Aim:** *To recognize Josiah's role in seeking to lead Judah to obey God's commands.*

STUDYING THE BIBLE

Outline and Summary
   I. King Josiah (2 Kings 22:1–2)
  II. The Book of the Law (2 Kings 22:3–20)
    1. Repair of the temple (22:3–7)
    2. Discovery of the book of the law (22:8–10)
    3. Josiah's initial response (22:11–13)
    4. Huldah's prophecy (22:14–20)
 III. Josiah's Religious Revival (2 Kings 23:1–20)
    1. Public reading of the book of the covenant (23:1–2)
    2. Renewing the covenant (23:3)
    3. Purification of religious life (23:4–20)

King Josiah did what was right in the sight of the Lord (22:1–2). He ordered extensive repairs to the temple (22:3–7). The book of the law was found in the temple and read to the king (22:8–10). Josiah was deeply disturbed because he realized that God's wrath was directed against the sins of Judah (22:11–13). The prophetess Huldah (HUHL duh) confirmed that God would punish Judah, but she commended Josiah (22:14–20). Josiah read the book to the people (23:1–2) and led them to renew their covenant with God (23:3). Then Josiah launched a vigorous campaign to root out all vestiges of past idolatry (23:4–20).

I. King Josiah (2 Kings 22:1–2)
Josiah's father Amon died young (2 Kings 21:19–26); therefore, Josiah was only eight years old when he became king. Like Hezekiah, Josiah proved to be a worthy descendant of their forefather David (compare verse 2 with 2 Kings 18:3).

II. The Book of the Law (2 Kings 22:3-20)

1. Repair of the temple (22:3-7). The temple had been desecrated by Manasseh during his long reign of fifty-five years (2 Kings 21:4-5,7). Josiah sent his scribe Shaphan (SHAY fan) to Hilkiah (hil KIGH uh) the high priest with a message about the temple. Josiah authorized extensive repairs to be made in the temple. Workmen were to be hired and the work done so thoroughly and honestly that no financial accounting would be needed.

2. Discovery of the book of the law (22:8-10). Shaphan reported to Hilkiah that he had found the book of the law in the house of the Lord. Shaphan reported to Josiah on the progress of the project to repair the temple, including the finding of a book. Shaphan read the book to Josiah.

3. Josiah's initial response (22:11-13). When Josiah heard the reading of the book of the law, he tore his clothes in grief and conviction. He dispatched Hilkiah, Shaphan, and others to inquire of the Lord about the plight of Judah. The king felt that God's wrath was directed against Judah for their failure to obey the commands of God in the book.

4. Huldah's prophecy (22:14-20). The king's delegation consulted Huldah, a prophetess, about the situation, and she delivered God's message. The Lord said that the sins of Judah had become so great that His wrath against Jerusalem could not be quenched. The Lord commended Josiah because he had humbled himself.

III. Josiah's Religious Revival (2 Kings 23:1-20)

1. Public reading of the book of the covenant (23:1-2)

1 And the king sent, and they gathered unto him all the elders of Judah and of Jerusalem.

2 And the king went up into the house of the Lord, and all the men of Judah and all the inhabitants of Jerusalem with him, and the priests, and the prophets, and all the people, both small and great: and he read in their ears all the words of the book of the covenant which was found in the house of the Lord.

When we read the account of 2 Kings 22-23, we wonder: "What exactly was the book that was found? How could it have been lost?" The book is described as "the book of the law" (22:8,11) and "the book of the covenant" (23:2). Although 2 Kings never tells us exactly what it was, we assume it was all or part of the first five books of the Bible.

Many Bible scholars think that the book—or actually, scroll—was from Deuteronomy. Three factors support this view. First, Josiah's words in 2 Kings 22:13 and Huldah's words in 2 Kings 22:19 sound like the curses against disobedience in Deuteronomy 28. Second, the words of covenant renewal in 2 Kings 23:3 ("with all their heart and all their soul") sound like Deuteronomy 6:5. Third, the attacks on idolatry and the positive aspects of Josiah's revival have parallels in Deuteronomy.

How could such a valuable document have become lost? Keep in mind that this was centuries before printing was invented. Scrolls were copied by hand. Thus there were fewer copies than in the age of printing. We should not overlook the influence of Manasseh's fifty-five-year reign, during which the evil king did everything possible to stamp out worship of the Lord and to replace it with various forms of idolatry. During those years, many believers were killed (2 Kings 21:16). Apparently copies of the Law were either destroyed or hidden during those dark years.

Josiah's first action, therefore, was to summon all the people to the temple to hear the king read from the newly found book of the covenant. Verse 2 elaborates on the groups who came to hear the reading. The congregation included not only the prophets and priests but also the inhabitants of Judah and of Jerusalem. The prominent citizens were there, but so were the common people.

Verse 2 is very much like what happened after the people returned from Babylonian (bab uh LOH nih un) exile, and Ezra read "the book of the law of Moses" to men, women, and children (Neh. 8:1–3). We know from the New Testament that synagogue services included the reading of the Scriptures (Luke 4:16–20; Acts 13:15). We also know that the great revivals of Christian history have included the public reading of the Word of God.

2. Renewing the covenant (23:3)

3 And the king stood by a pillar, and made a covenant before the Lord, to walk after the Lord, and to keep his commandments and his testimonies and his statutes with all their heart and all their soul, to perform the words of this covenant that were written in this book. And all the people stood to the covenant.

The reading of the book of the covenant was followed by a ceremony in which Josiah led the people in renewing the covenant. The reading of the book had shown them the distinctive covenant that God had made with the descendants of Israel. The people of Israel were called to a distinctive faith in the one true God and to a distinctive way of life involving obedience to His commands. The renewal ceremony emphasized the obligation of the people to walk in the Lord's way by obeying all His commands with all their heart and soul.

No generation of Israelites could afford to take the covenant for granted. Each generation had to commit themselves anew to the covenant. And often the same generation had to renew their covenant relationship and obligations. Indeed the Book of Deuteronomy tells how Moses led the second generation out of Egypt to renew the covenant that God had made with their parents at Mount Sinai (SIGH nay ih).

Under the new covenant, each person must accept or reject God's covenant. Our response involves trust and obedience. And because the heart of this covenant is a personal relationship with God, such a relationship must be expressed daily and renewed continually.

3. Purification of religious life (23:4–20)

4 And the king commanded Hilkiah the high priest, and the priests of the second order, and the keepers of the door, to bring forth out of the temple of the Lord all the vessels that were made for Baal, and for the grove, and for all the host of heaven: and he burned them without Jerusalem in the fields of Kidron [KID ruhn] and carried the ashes of them unto Bethel.

5 And he put down the idolatrous priests, whom the kings of

Judah had ordained to burn incense in the high places in the cities of Judah, and in the places round about Jerusalem; them also that burned incense unto Baal, to the sun, and to the moon, and to the planets, and to all the host of heaven.

6 And he brought out the grove from the house of the LORD, without Jerusalem, unto the brook Kidron, and burned it at the brook Kidron, and stamped it small to powder, and cast the powder thereof upon the graves of the children of the people.

7 And he brake down the houses of the sodomites, that were by the house of the Lord, where the women wove hangings for the grove.

8 And he brought all the priests out of the cities of Judah, and defiled the high places where the priests had burned incense, from Geba [GHEE buh] to Beersheba [Bee ehr SHE buh].

These verses reveal the terrible extent of the idolatry that afflicted Judah and the zeal of Josiah in trying to destroy it. Much of the idolatry had to do with Baal worship. The word *grove* is literally "Asherah" (ASH uh ruh), the name of the female god of Baal religion. The word is sometimes translated "Ashtaroth" (ASH tuh rahth; Judg. 2:13; 1 Sam. 7:3–4). She was often worshiped as an image. Baal worship was a fertility religion that involved male and female prostitutes as an integral part of the religion.

Another form of idolatry involved worship of the sun, moon, and stars. Whereas Baal worship had its roots in Sidon (SIGH duhn) and Canaan (KAY nuhn), the worship of the heavenly host came from Assyria (uh SIRH ih uh) and Babylonia (bab uh LOH nih uh). When Manasseh built altars for such, he showed his subjection to Assyria. By the time of Josiah, the power of Assyria was waning; and the zealous young king could assert his independence by destroying the altars of Assyrian worship.

The idols were not only found in the local shrines ("high places") scattered throughout the land, but had taken over the temple itself. Josiah removed the altars of Baal worship and Assyrian worship from both the temple and the high places. He deposed the priests who had served at these pagan altars. He burned the image of Asherah at Kidron, pounded it to powder, and further defiled it by sprinkling the powder on graves—which the people considered unclean. Josiah destroyed the houses of the male prostitutes of Baal, which adjoined the temple. Josiah defiled all the high places where idolatry had been practiced.

Josiah zealously set out to destroy all the idols and to defile all the pagan places of worship in Judah and Israel. This included the valley where child sacrifice had been practiced (v. 10). He removed horses and chariots used in sun worship (v. 11). He destroyed idols set up by previous kings, including some that went back to the time of Solomon (vv. 12–14). Josiah also defiled the altar at Bethel, which had led to the doom of the Northern Kingdom (vv. 15–18). He destroyed the high places in Israel and killed the priests who had served there (vv. 19–20).

APPLYING THE BIBLE

1. **Early commitment to Christ.** One day in a seminary evangelism class, Professor Ray Summers asked all those who had accepted Christ

before they were ten to raise their hands. By far the majority of those in the very large class raised their hands. Summers then stated that he and his wife prayed daily that their children would receive Christ as their Savior at the first recognition of their sin and guilt, not spending even one day in rebellion against God. What a prayer for parents to pray and what a marvelous ideal! But, unfortunately, the majority of parents today do not recognize their own need of Jesus let alone that of their children. To be sure, the children must be dealt with cautiously, but Solomon's admonition is still the best advice that can be given on behalf of an early commitment to Jesus: "Remember now thy Creator in the days of thy youth, while the evil days come not, nor the years draw nigh, when thou shalt say, I have no pleasure in them" (Eccl. 12:1).

"Good King Josiah" was one of those who sought the Lord early. Crowned king at the age of eight (2 Kings 22:1), he "began to seek after the God of David" in the eighth year of his reign (2 Chron. 34:3).

2. The lost Bible. The late Baptist historian Dr. Robert A. Baker in his book A Summary of Christian History writes: "Pope Innocent III (1198–1216) denounced the translation of the Scriptures to the language of the people, and the possession of Scriptures in the vernacular tongue was looked on as heresy."[1] But the word of God cannot be bound! Through the work of immortal, sacrificial believers such as Wycliffe, Tyndale, Luther and others, the Bibles began to be put in the hands of Europeans all across the continent. And reformation resulted!

The same thing happened in the eighteenth year of Josiah's reign when a "book of the law" was found while repairs were being made on the temple (2 Kings 23:1). Scholars believe the lost book contained portions of Deuteronomy that called Israel to exclusive loyalty to Jehovah. And again, as the Scriptures were read, reformation resulted (23:1–25).

What do you suppose a diligent daily reading of God's Word could mean to our homes and nation today?

3. One who suffered to put the Scriptures in the hands of common people. We take our Bible for granted. It's easy to own a Bible and we do not suffer for having one. But it was not always so. Many believers, whose crime was nothing more than loving the Word of God, were persecuted by the Roman Catholic Church. One of them was William Tyndale.

Born in England in 1494, Tyndale was one of the leaders of the Protestant Reformation. Determined to give the Bible to the people, he was forced into exile in 1535. With a bounty on his head, he taught himself Hebrew and worked six days a week from dawn to dusk for eleven years translating the Scriptures. Finally, the work was completed and Tyndale's finished Bible was smuggled into England. Tyndale was caught in 1536, and Henry VIII condemned him to be hanged. Before Tyndale went to the gallows, he prayed: "Lord, open the eyes of the king of England."

God answered his prayer, and in 1539 King Henry sent a royal decree encouraging all printers and publishers to publish the Scriptures for "the free and liberal use of the Bible in our native tongue."

Like Josiah of old, Tyndale was faithful to the Word of God. Pick up your Bible, look at it. Remember that Josiah, Tyndale, and others have given it to you at great cost. Then ask yourself: "How can I do less than love it and follow it?"

4. Keeping the Commandments. An early day preacher was once confronted by one of the sophisticated ladies of his congregation, so it is told, who rebuked him for introducing new "rituals" into their worship service.

"And what new ritual is that?" asked the pastor. "Oh, I hear that you are now reading the Ten Commandments in the service," sniffed the parishioner.

"Is that all you heard?" asked the preacher. "But you need to understand that we have added a ritual that goes even further than that," replied the pastor. "I am telling our people that we ought to live by those Commandments."

When the lost book of the Law was discovered, Josiah not only read the Scriptures to the people but told them they must keep them.

The Ten Commandments are not ten suggestions. God still commands us to live by them in our lost, pagan world today.

TEACHING THE BIBLE

▶ *Main Idea:* God calls on us to remove idolatrous practices from our communities.

▶ *Suggested Teaching Aim:* To encourage members to take a positive role in helping to eliminate those things that are displeasing to God in their community

A TEACHING OUTLINE

1. Use a collection of objects to introduce the lesson.
2. Use charts, lecture, and group discussion to study the Bible.
3. Use brainstorming to apply the Bible to life.

Introduce the Bible Study

Collect several objects, pictures, or relics that could be worshiped or are worshiped by certain religions. Include items that your class could worship (job, family, money, and so forth). Ask members which of these they worship. Point out that at times even good things (job, family) can become idols. Suggest that today's lesson will encourage them to take a positive role in helping to eliminate those things that are displeasing to God in their community.

Search for Biblical Truth

Enlist a member to present a monologue in which the person describes the events in the introduction and points I and II. If you choose not to do this, summarize these events in a brief lecture.

Ask a volunteer to read 2 Kings 23:1–2 and explain Josiah's actions. Explain that many Bible scholars suggest three reasons why they believe the scroll was Deuteronomy. On a chalkboard or a large sheet of paper, make the following chart:

	2 Kings	Deuteronomy
1.	22:13,19	28:15–68
2.	23:3	6:5
3.	23:4,6,7,14	7:5; 12:3; 16:21

Ask half of the class to look at the references in 2 Kings and the other half to look at the references in Deuteronomy. Point out that the references in number 3 refer only to the abolition of the groves or Asherim.

Using "Studying the Bible," explain how such an important document could have been lost. Call on a volunteer to read 23:3 and point out the people's renewal of the covenant.

DISCUSS: What value do periodic covenant-renewal services such as revivals have for believers? How can we keep our covenant with God and not let it get broken? What role does the Bible play in helping us eliminate idolatrous practices from our lives?

Ask members silently to read 23:4–8 and, based on what the people destroyed, list what kinds of idolatrous worship the people engaged in. (We can assume that because Josiah destroyed the groves or Asherah [or Asherim (plural)] they worshiped Asherah.) List these on a chalkboard or a large sheet of paper in one column. Then opposite each idolatrous action, list what Josiah and his reformation did to this practice. Some practices/actions are given below, but your members may find others:

Idolatrous Practice	Josiah's Actions
Worshiped Asherah	Destroyed her images
Worshiped sun, moon, and stars	Destroyed images
Worshiped golden calf at Bethel	Defiled image by scattering ashes
Idolatrous priests burned incense	Removed priests
Worshiped Asherah in temple	Burned image in Kidron
Used male prostitutes	Destroyed prostitutes' house
Worshiped at high places	Defiled high places

Give the Truth a Personal Focus

Ask members to list some idolatrous practices they find in their lives and in their community. Write these on a chalkboard or a large sheet of paper.

Ask: What can we do to eliminate idolatrous practices in our lives? What can we do to lead out in eliminating idolatrous practices in our community?

Encourage members to choose both personal and community projects and set some goals that will help them reach these. Suggest that faithfulness to Bible study will help them as it did Josiah.

---

1 Robert A. Baker, *A Summary of Christian History*, rev. ed. by John M. Landers (Nashville: Broadman & Holman, 1994), 184.

Hearing God's Call

Basic Passage: Jeremiah 1
Focal Passages: Jeremiah 1:4–10,14–17

Jeremiah was the key prophet of God during the final years of Judah. For over four decades, he spoke God's word concerning the coming fall of Jerusalem. However, as his messages of judgment were being fulfilled, he became a prophet of hope—a hope that looked beyond the exile. The Book of Jeremiah begins with the account of God's call to Jeremiah and of Jeremiah's response.

▶ ▶ ▶ ▶ ▶ ▶ ▶ ▶ ▶ **Study Aim:** *To describe God's call to Jeremiah and his response.*

STUDYING THE BIBLE

Outline and Summary
 I. Introduction to the Book of Jeremiah (Jer. 1:1–3)
 II. God's Call to Jeremiah (Jer. 1:4–19)
   1. Set apart to be a prophet (vv. 4–5)
   2. Jeremiah's sense of inadequacy (v. 6)
   3. Equipped and commissioned (vv. 7–10)
   4. Vision of an almond branch (vv. 11–12)
   5. Vision of a boiling pot (vv. 13–16)
   6. Challenged and reassured (vv. 17–19)

The word of the Lord came to Jeremiah (vv. 1–3). God set him apart to be a prophet before he was born (vv. 4–5). Jeremiah said that he was too young to speak for God (v. 6). God touched his mouth and commanded him to speak His word (vv. 7–10). Jeremiah saw an almond branch, reminding him that God was watching over His word (vv. 11–12). Jeremiah saw a boiling pot, representing the coming of invaders (vv. 13–16). God challenged Jeremiah to speak without fear because God would be with him (vv. 17–19).

I. Introduction to the Book of Jeremiah (Jer. 1:1–3)

Jeremiah was the son of a priest. He grew up in Anathoth (AN uh thawth), in the portion of the land where Benjamin's descendants settled years before. The word of God came to him in the thirteenth year of Josiah (joh SIGH uh) or 627 B.C. His prophetic ministry continued until the eleventh year of Zedekiah (zed uh KIGH uh) or 586 B.C., when Jerusalem was captured.

II. God's Call to Jeremiah (Jer. 1:4–19)

1. Set apart to be a prophet (vv. 4–5)
   4 Then the word of the Lord came unto me, saying,
   5 Before I formed thee in the belly I knew thee; and before thou camest forth out of the womb I sanctified thee, and I or-

dained thee a prophet unto the nations.

Verse 4 uses terms that are found throughout the Book of Jeremiah. Over and over, Jeremiah testified, "The word of the Lord came unto me." Jeremiah did not decide on his own to be a prophet, nor did he make up his own messages. From his initial call until his final prophecy, Jeremiah was someone to whom God's word came and who in turn declared that word to others. At the beginning of his written prophecies, the prophet told how he came to be a man controlled by the word of the Lord.

Actually, the beginning was well before the time when Jeremiah first heard God's call. God's call was the expression of a purpose that extended back before Jeremiah was born. The word *formed* was used in Genesis 2:7 to describe God's creation of Adam from the dust of the earth. Jeremiah 1:5 uses the same word to describe what takes place within a mother's womb as a new life is created by the hand of God.

God not only "formed" Jeremiah within his mother's womb; the Lord "knew" him. The word denotes personal knowledge. God did not first notice Jeremiah after he was born and showed distinctive personal traits. God created him and knew him from before he was born. Jeremiah's awareness of this divine purpose for his life helped him persevere through the difficult years of his ministry. Jeremiah realized that God had been at work to endow and shape him for the task to which God called him.

In addition to "formed" and "knew," verse 5 uses two other words to describe God's call of Jeremiah. The word *sanctified* literally means to be set apart. God had set him apart to be a special person with a special mission from God. He was consecrated to be a holy person with a holy mission.

The word *appointed* carries the idea of being "given." The Lord had given Jeremiah as a prophet to the nations. Although his message focused on Judah, Jeremiah's word from God often included other nations. Neither Judah nor the nations recognized Jeremiah as a gift of God to them.

2. Jeremiah's sense of inadequacy (v. 6)

6 Then said I, Ah, Lord God! behold, I cannot speak: for I am a child.

The word *child* generally was used to refer to a young, unmarried man. Thus Jeremiah was not what we would call a child, but a single young adult, perhaps even a teenager. Unlike our society, where younger people often have great influence, the world of Jeremiah listened primarily to the words of married people of more maturity. Older people were considered to be especially wise. Thus Jeremiah responded to God's call by noting that he lacked the maturity to speak in such a way that people would pay attention.

The part of Jeremiah's response about his inability to speak sounds like what Moses said when the Lord called him. Moses protested, "O my Lord, I am not eloquent, . . . but I am slow of speech, and of a slow tongue" (Exod. 4:10). Moses based his inadequacy on being unable to speak eloquently. Jeremiah based his inadequacy on his youth.

When we compare verse 6 to Isaiah 6:8, we see that Jeremiah was not an eager volunteer like Isaiah. On the other hand, Jeremiah's words do not reflect an unwillingness to answer God's call. They do reveal a deep sense of personal inadequacy for the task. Verse 6 also is the first of many candid prayers of Jeremiah. The Book of Jeremiah contains many dialogues between God and Jeremiah. Both Jeremiah and God spoke to each other with total honesty.

3. Equipped and commissioned (vv. 7–10)

7 But the Lord said unto me, Say not, I am a child: for thou shalt go to all that I shall send thee, and whatsoever I command thee thou shalt speak.

8 Be not afraid of their faces: for I am with thee to deliver thee, saith the Lord.

9 Then the Lord put forth his hand, and touched my mouth. And the Lord said unto me, Behold, I have put my words in thy mouth.

10 See, I have this day set thee over the nations and over the kingdoms, to root out, and to pull down, and to destroy, and to throw down, to build, and to plant.

God told Jeremiah not to see his youth as a reason not to obey. Instead, Jeremiah was to go to those to whom God sent him and to speak what God told him to speak. Jeremiah was not to be worried with how people might respond to his words; instead he was to obey God and leave the outcome in the hands of God.

What God told Jeremiah to do was easier said than done. How was the young man to be able to speak to his sinful generation? God told him not to fear the menacing looks and threatening words of people. Where was he to find his courage? The Lord promised to be with him. "Fear not: for I am with thee" (Isa. 43:5) is a recurring theme in the Bible. The assurance of the abiding presence of God is the antidote for the many fears that rise up before us and within us.

One sign of the Lord's presence with Jeremiah was that the Lord put His words into the prophet's mouth. As a sign of this, the Lord touched the prophet's mouth with His hand. The Lord sent an angel to touch the lips of Isaiah for cleansing (Isa. 6:5–7). This prepared Isaiah to hear and respond to God's call. In Jeremiah's case, God touched his lips to reassure the young man that God would use him to speak His words. Thus Jeremiah did not need to worry about his youth and inexperience as a speaker. God would be with him and would speak through him.

God was going to endow the young prophet with authority over nations and kingdoms. He would be God's representative to people of power and position. His task was described in six symbolic words; four of them negative and two, positive. Most of Jeremiah's ministry was pronouncing judgment on evil. This is depicted as rooting out, pulling down, destroying, and throwing down. Jeremiah did not choose such a ministry. He was chosen for it by God because the times required it. As judgment began to fall, God began to give more hopeful messages to the prophet. This is depicted as building and planting.

4. Vision of an almond branch (vv. 11–12). God called Jeremiah's attention to an almond branch. The almond tree was among the first plants to awake from winter. The Lord told Jeremiah that He was awake and watching over His word to perform it.

5. Vision of a boiling pot (vv. 13–16). Then God called Jeremiah's attention to a boiling pot that faced from the north and thus was prepared to overflow toward the south (v. 13).

> **14 Then the Lord said unto me, Out of the north an evil shall break forth upon all the inhabitants of the land.**
>
> **15 For, lo, I will call all the families of the kingdoms of the north, saith the Lord; and they shall come, and they shall set every one his throne at the entering of the gates of Jerusalem, and against all the walls thereof round about, and against the cities of Judah.**
>
> **16 And I will utter my judgments against them touching all their wickedness, who have forsaken me, and have burned incense unto other gods, and worshipped the works of their own hands.**

The boiling pot was a sign that enemies from the North would bring judgment on Jerusalem and the cities of Judah. Jeremiah often warned of invaders from the North. This sign, which came as part of Jeremiah's call, did not identify the invaders by name.

Jeremiah's call came at about the time that the Assyrian (uh SIHR ih uhn) Empire crumbled. A number of powers were vying to become the next superpower. Eventually Babylonia (bab uh LOH nih uh) came out on top. Later in Jeremiah's ministry, he identified the Babylonians as the instruments of divine judgment on Judah.

The Bible accurately represents the events of history when they intersected events in God's plan of redemption. The Bible interprets history from this perspective: God is the sovereign Lord of all nations. He moves in the affairs of history to accomplish His divine purpose. One example of this was God's use of the Babylonians to punish the people of Judah for their persistent idolatry. The Babylonians were not aware that they were instruments in the hands of God, but they were nonetheless.

6. Challenged and reassured (vv. 17–19)

> **17 Thou therefore gird up thy loins, and arise, and speak unto them all that I command thee: be not dismayed at their faces, lest I confound thee before them.**

The men of Jeremiah's day wore long robes. When they prepared to work or run, they gathered up the robes about their waists and tied them. This is the image behind the frequent use in the Bible of the words "gird up thy loins." People today sometimes say, "Roll up your sleeves." Both expressions mean the same thing: get ready for vigorous exercise or hard work.

The word *arise* was a call to get up and begin the task. God had called, equipped, and commissioned Jeremiah. Now was the time for him to begin to do what God had called him to do.

The last part of verse 17 expands on the words "be not afraid of their faces" in verse 8. This warning against fear implies that Jeremiah would face many scary situations and people.

Verses 18–19 spell this out more clearly. Everyone in Judah was going to oppose him. This included kings, princes, priests, and all the people. Later chapters record their ridicule, threats, and persecution of Jeremiah. He would face more than enough to strike terror into the heart of a young man listening to God's call. God did not hide this from Jeremiah. Instead, God warned him ahead of time. However, God repeated the gist of verse 8.

First of all, Jeremiah was not to be frightened or dismayed by the angry faces and threatening words and actions of those to whom he spoke. God warned the prophet that if he gave way to fear, God would let him reap the consequences of his fear. However, God said that there was no need to fear. God promised, "I am with thee, saith the Lord, to deliver thee" (v. 19).

APPLYING THE BIBLE

1. Jeremiah was the foremost man in the seventh century B.C., so says Old Testament scholar John R. Sampey. Jeremiah was called to be a prophet to Judah in the thirteenth year of the reign of Judah's great king Josiah (1:2).

2. God's knowledge of and call to Jeremiah before he was born. One of the strongest, clearest verses in the Old Testament that ought to empower believers in their relentless opposition to the hideous sin of abortion appears in vv. 4–5 of our lesson today. Read it carefully.

Will the abortionists be held innocent on Judgment Day who have mutilated and murdered those "formed," "known," "sanctified," and "ordained" by God before they were born?

3. A common problem. Fear is a problem to us all—even to Jeremiah (v. 6). When God called Jeremiah to his prophetic office, he shrank back in fear from the responsibility.

An ancient Arabian legend tells of two travelers meeting outside a city. One was a hideous-looking creature who, when asked by the other traveler his name and where he was going, replied: "My name is Pestilence, and I am going into the city to take five thousand lives."

Sometime later, the two met again and the traveler said to Pestilence, "You lied to me, for you took fifty thousand lives."

"No," Pestilence said, "I lied not to you. I took only five thousand lives, the rest died from fear of me!"

Courage is not the absence of fear; rather, it is going on to do one's duty in spite of fear. And Jeremiah must be credited with a great deal of courage to assume the mantle of leadership that cost him so much.

What is your greatest fear? Tell it to Jesus, for He is good for even that!

4. Again' it! Calvin Coolidge was a shy, silent man who had little to say. He served as our president in the mid–1920s. Years ago, the story goes, a man met Coolidge on his way home from church. "Where you been, Cal?" he asked, and Coolidge replied, "Church." " What did the preacher preach on, Cal?" the neighbor asked. "Sin," Coolidge replied. "And what did he say about it?" the neighbor asked. "Said he was again' it!" and Coolidge walked on.

Jeremiah let the people of Judah know that God was against their sin. The task of every preacher is to let people know that God hates their sins but loves them with an everlasting love.

5. "You have been warned." The noted British minister William Barclay, whose books line the studies of thousands of preachers today, tells about a stretch of road under repair in the north of England. Warning signs were posted on the dangerous, steep road with a sharp bend. The last sign read, "You have been warned!"

Judah had been warned by the prophets, including Jeremiah, that her sins were going to cost her everything, but rather than heeding the warnings, the nation plunged on into chaos.

Warning people and pleading for them to repent were the first message Jesus preached. And they are the preacher's primary message needed in our wicked world today.

6. The prophet's work can be disappointing. It is told that Billy Graham was once flying on a crowded plane when a drunken man got up, walked back to Graham, stuck out his hand and said: "Put 'er there, Billy. I'm really glad to see you. You have no idea how much your sermons have helped me!"

The preacher's work is often discouraging. We don't see the results we would like to see. Jeremiah faithfully declared God's word to the people of Judah, but they would have none of it. And the hardness of their hearts cost them dearly when they were carried off into the Babylonian exile.

Jeremiah's life seems like a complete failure, but not so. Anyone who stands against sin and for righteousness is always an immense success.

TEACHING THE BIBLE

▶ *Main Idea:* God calls people to serve Him in difficult days.
▶ *Suggested Teaching Aim:* To encourage adults to respond to God's call.

A TEACHING OUTLINE

1. Use an illustration to introduce the Bible study.
2. Use lecture and group discussion to guide the Bible study.
3. Use questions to apply the Bible.

Introduce the Bible Study

Use "The prophet's work can be disappointing" from "Applying the Bible" to introduce the lesson.

Search for Biblical Truth

IN ADVANCE, prepare a poster with the outline of the background passage on it and place paper strips over each point. Prepare a lecture covering the material in "Studying the Bible."

Uncover "I. Introduction to the Book of Jeremiah (Jer. 1:1–3)." IN ADVANCE, enlist a member to prepare a brief report on Jeremiah based on the *Holman Bible Dictionary* or summarize the material in "Studying the Bible" under this point.

Uncover "II. God's Call to Jeremiah (Jer. 1:4–19)" and "1. Set apart to be a prophet (1:4–5)." Explain the following: "The Word of the Lord came unto me" (1:4), "formed," "knew," "sanctified," and "appointed" (1:5).

DISCUSS: What does God's knowledge of Jeremiah before birth say about God's concern for all people? What purpose did Jeremiah's awareness of God's divine purpose have?

Uncover "2. Jeremiah's sense of inadequacy (1:6)." Explain the meaning of the word *child* (1:6). Compare and contrast the call of Jeremiah with the calls of Moses and Isaiah.

DISCUSS: Why does God call certain people to His ministry? Did Jeremiah have an opportunity to refuse? Do we?

Uncover "3. Equipped and commissioned (1:7–10)." Point out the two fold warning ("Say not" and "be not afraid") and the six fold mission ("Root," "pull," "destroy," "throw," "build," and "plant").

DISCUSS: Would we be more likely to listen to a young evangelist or an older one? How can we tell if God is speaking through either? How do you think Jeremiah felt about his ministry?

Uncover "4. Vision of an almond branch (1:11–12)," and relate the meaning based on the paragraph in "Studying the Bible."

Uncover "5. Vision of a boiling pot (1:13–16." Ask members to name some symbols the prophets used to get their message across. Point out that Jeremiah here used a pot sitting in a fire and filled with boiling water. The pot was tipped so that when the water started to boil, it spilled over. Explain the meaning of the symbol.

DISCUSS: Why does God allow evil people to defeat good people? What does this say about God's control of all the nations of the earth? Do you believe God is in control of all the nations of the earth today? Why?

Uncover the last point: "6. Challenged and reassured (1:17–19)." Explain "gird up thy loins." Point out the four instructions to Jeremiah in 1:17: "gird up," "arise," "speak," and "be not dismayed." Point out that it was now time for Jeremiah to get on with his task.

DISCUSS: Why does God call us to tasks in which people will oppose and ridicule us? What does God do to prepare us for our tasks?

Give the Truth a Personal Focus

Ask: Does God still call us today as He called Jeremiah? Has He called you to some task?

Remind members that God still calls people to difficult tasks. Ask members seriously to consider God's call for their lives. Pray that all will respond as God calls.

Proclaiming God's Word

Basic Passage: Jeremiah 7
Focal Passage: Jeremiah 7:1–15

J eremiah 7 records a memorable example of the prophet's proclamation of God's word. As we noted in studying Jeremiah's call,
God called him to proclaim His word to people who responded
by rejecting the word and persecuting the prophet. At times in his difficult ministry, Jeremiah tried to refrain from speaking God's word.
However, Jeremiah testified that he had to proclaim God's word because it was like a fire in his bones (Jer. 20:9).

▶ ▶ ▶ ▶ **Study Aim:** *To summarize the main points of Jeremiah's
temple sermon.*

STUDYING THE BIBLE

Outline and Summary
  I. Jeremiah's Temple Sermon (Jer. 7:1–15)
   1. Setting and theme of the sermon (vv. 1–4)
   2. What God expects (vv. 5–7)
   3. Hypocritical worship and sinful living (vv. 8–11)
   4. Sure judgment (vv. 12–15)
  II. Jeremiah Told Not to Pray for the People (Jer. 7:16–20)
  III. God Demands Obedience (Jer. 7:21–34)
   1. God's command to Israel (vv. 21–23)
   2. Israel's persistent disobedience (vv. 24–31)
   3. Terrible judgment (vv. 32–34)

Speaking at the gate of the temple, Jeremiah spoke God's word,
which called the people to amend their ways and to cease chanting
their false assurance about the temple (vv. 1–4). The Lord
promised that if they amended their ways by practicing justice and
ceasing idolatry, they would continue to dwell in the land (vv.
5–7). Unfortunately, the people broke God's commandments and
went to the temple like a band of robbers retreating to the safety of
their den (vv. 8–11). As God destroyed Shiloh (SHIGH loh) and Israel, so He would destroy Judah for their refusal to hear God's persistent call (vv. 12–15). The people had become so wicked that
God forbade Jeremiah to pray for them (vv. 16–20). God's basic
command to Israel had been to obey His voice (vv. 21–23), but Israel had continually disobeyed God (vv. 24–28). They had committed such abominations (vv. 29–31) that nothing remained but
terrible judgment (vv. 32–34).

I. Jeremiah's Temple Sermon
(Jer. 7:1-15)

1. Setting and theme of the sermon (vv. 1–4)

1 The word that came to Jeremiah from the Lord, saying,

2 Stand in the gate of the Lord's house, and proclaim there this word, and say, Hear the word of the Lord, all ye of Judah, that enter in at these gates to worship the Lord.

Jeremiah took his stand at one of the entrances to the temple. From this point, he was able to speak to the people in the outer court as they prepared to go through their acts of worship.

Most Bible students think that Jeremiah 26:1 gives the setting for Jeremiah's temple sermon. Josiah (joh SIGH uh) had tried to revive worship in the temple. Jeremiah had received his call a few years before Josiah began his reforms (Jer. 1:1; 2 Kings 22:3). Thus the prophet was aware of what Josiah tried to do. Jeremiah was already a prophet when Josiah was killed in battle, when Jehoahaz (jih HOH uh haz) reigned for three months, and when Jehoiakim became king (2 Kings 23:29–37). Jeremiah 26:1 says that Jeremiah spoke in the temple at the beginning of the reign of Jehoiakim (jih HOY uh kim), which was in 609 B.C.

3 Thus saith the LORD of hosts, the God of Israel, Amend your ways and your doings, and I will cause you to dwell in this place.

4 Trust ye not in lying words, saying, The temple of the Lord, The temple of the Lord, The temple of the Lord, are these.

The word *amend* means to do good. Repentance means turning from sin and with God's help beginning to do good. God promised the people of Judah that He would allow them to continue to dwell in the promised land if they amended their habits and actions.

The Lord warned them not to trust in lying words about the temple. The content of this false trust is described further in verse 9. Verse 4 says that the lie took the form of a chant that repeated "The temple of the Lord." They assumed that the temple was protection against whatever threatened them.

Jeremiah was by no means the only person in the land who professed to be a prophet of the Lord. The other "prophets" proclaimed a different message than Jeremiah. They preached peace and security for God's people. They based this on God's deliverance of Jerusalem from the Assyrians during the time of Isaiah and Hezekiah (hez ih KIGH uh; see the lesson for September 1). Thus when Jeremiah warned of judgment on Judah and the destruction of the temple, the other prophets assured the people that God would never allow anything bad to happen to His people and to His holy house.

2. What God expects (vv. 5–7)

5 For if ye thoroughly amend your ways and your doings; if ye thoroughly execute judgment between a man and his neighbour;

6 If ye oppress not the stranger, the fatherless, and the widow, and shed not innocent blood in this place, neither walk after other gods to your hurt:

7 Then will I cause you to dwell in this place, in the land that I gave to your fathers, for ever and ever.

Verses 5–7 expand on the meaning of verse 3. In Hebrew, these are one long sentence with several "if" clauses, which lead up to a promise. If Israel met the conditions stated in the "if" clauses, God promised that they could continue to dwell in the land.

The "if" clauses in verses 5–6 further define what ways and doings needed to be amended. The last part of verse 5 shows that God expected His people to practice justice (the meaning of "judgment") in their dealings with other people.

The first part of verse 6 reflects special concern for foreigners, orphans, and widows. These groups were exploited by unscrupulous people and ignored by selfish people. The Law commanded the Israelites not to mistreat these dependent groups (Deut. 24:17–18). The prophets repeated this command: "Learn to do well, seek judgment, relieve the oppressed, judge the fatherless, plead for the widow" (Isa. 1:17).

The warning against shedding innocent blood in the temple included actual murders in the temple (such as the incident in 2 Chron. 24:20–21; Matt. 23:35 refers to this incident). These words also applied to those who came to the temple with hands stained by innocent blood (vv. 9–10; Isa. 1:15).

Verse 7 also contains a warning against the Israelites' besetting sin of idolatry, which they had sometimes practiced even in the temple (2 Kings 21:3–5).

3. Hypocritical worship and sinful living (vv. 8–11)

8 Behold, ye trust in lying words, that cannot profit.

9 Will ye steal, murder, and commit adultery, and swear falsely, and burn incense unto Baal, and walk after other gods whom ye know not;

10 And come and stand before me in this house, which is called by my name, and say, We are delivered to do all these abominations?

11 Is this house, which is called by my name, become a den of robbers in your eyes? Behold, even I have seen it, saith the Lord.

Verses 8–11 expand on the warning against false trust in the temple in verse 4. Both passages show that the people had put their trust in lying words about the temple. Two piercing questions in verses 9–11 reveal how they deceived themselves and perverted the purpose of the temple.

The first question in verses 9–10 shows what the lie was. They had convinced themselves that they could practice the worst of sins and still be safe—as long as they continued to go through the motions of worship in the temple. Their sins included breaking the Sixth (murder), Seventh (adultery), Eighth (stealing), and Ninth (false swearing) Commandments. They also broke the first two Commandments by their worship of other gods.

You can almost hear the shock and anger in the prophet's voice as he condemned this unbelievable hypocrisy. They committed these terrible sins. Then they came to the temple, which was supposed to represent the holy name of God. They said that their faithfulness in temple observances protected them from harm and thus freed them to continue their abominations!

The question in verse 11 asks if they were not thinking of the temple the same way that robbers thought of their den. A robbers' den was thought of as a safe place to stay between crimes.

4. Sure judgment (vv. 12–15)

12 But go ye now unto my place which was in Shiloh, where I set my name at the first, and see what I did to it for the wickedness of my people Israel.

13 And now, because ye have done all these works, saith the Lord, and I spake unto you, rising up early and speaking, but ye heard not; and I called you, but ye answered not;

14 Therefore will I do unto this house, which is called by my name, wherein ye trust, and unto the place which I gave to you and to your fathers, as I have done to Shiloh.

15 And I will cast you out of my sight, as I have cast out all your brethren, even the whole seed of Ephraim [EE frih uhm].

Shiloh had been an important place of worship during Israel's early history. Joshua chose Shiloh as the resting place for the tabernacle (Josh. 18:1). It was still there during the time of Eli (1 Sam. 1:3). Eli's two evil sons took the ark of the covenant from Shiloh when the Israelites fought the Philistines (fih LISS teens). The people thought that the presence of the ark would ensure victory for them (1 Sam. 4:3). Instead, the ark was captured and the Israelites defeated (1 Sam. 4:11). Judging from Jeremiah's words, the place of worship at Shiloh was destroyed.

Speaking through Jeremiah, the Lord accused the Israelites of putting their trust in the temple in the same way their forefathers had trusted in the ark from Shiloh. God said that He would destroy the temple as surely as He had destroyed Shiloh, when it became a place of hypocritical worship. Verse 13 describes the persistent but futile entreaties of the Lord to His people. They had refused His every plea. Nothing remained but destruction like that of Shiloh and of the Northern Kingdom (Ephraim).

II. Jeremiah Told Not to Pray for the People (Jer. 7:16–20)

God took the drastic step of ordering Jeremiah not to intercede anymore for Judah. Their sins had caused them to pass beyond the point of no return. Ahead lay sure judgment.

III. God Demands Obedience (Jer. 7:21–34)

1. God's command to Israel (vv. 21–23). The Lord reminded the people that His basic command was not to offer burnt offerings, but to obey the Lord.

2. Israel's persistent disobedience (vv. 24–31). The history of Israel had been a history of disobeying God. Since the deliverance from Egypt, God had sent prophets calling the people to repent and obey, but Israel had continually hardened their hearts. Judah should prepare for judgment because of such abominations as idol worship in the temple and child sacrifice.

3. Terrible judgment (vv. 32–34). The valley where children had been sacrificed would become a place where evildoers would be slaughtered. All sounds of joy would disappear from the desolate land.

APPLYING THE BIBLE

1. Tall enough to reach heaven. A church elder once came to his bishop requesting that he send a preacher to serve among them. The bishop asked, "And how big a man do you want?" The elder replied: "We do not care about his size, but we want a preacher who is tall enough to reach heaven on his knees!"

Such a man was Jeremiah in Judah's most-trying hours. Still the nation did not listen to him or heed his divine warnings.

2. Only outward obedience. A little boy who was standing in his chair at the dinner table was told by his mother to sit down. But he paid her no mind even as she insisted that he sit down. Finally, she plopped him down in the chair and he blurted through tears, "I may be sitting down on the outside, but I'm standing on the inside!"

That was the same kind of disobedience that marked Judah. She involved herself in the outward adornments of serving God, but in her heart she rebelled against what God commanded her to be and do (vv. 8–12).

3. Friends of Jesus? Dr. R. A. Torrey (1856–1927) was a Congregationalist preacher, teacher, and evangelist who made a great impact for Christ. One evening Torrey was told that a minister's son was to be in the large meeting Torrey was conducting. Although the young man was a professing Christian, Torrey was told the young man's life gave little indication of it.

Meeting him at the door, Torrey asked, "Are you a friend of Jesus?" Quickly the young man replied, "I consider myself to be a friend of Jesus." To which Torrey replied: "Ye are my friends if you do whatsoever I command you." The young man's eyes fell and he replied, "If those are the conditions, I suppose I am not."

Loudly and frequently, in their temple worship, Judah claimed to be a friend of God, but her works denied her profession (vv. 1–11).

Are you a friend of Jesus?

4. Partial obedience. Adoniram Judson was a pioneer missionary to Burma. When Judson finished seminary, he was offered a call from a fashionable church in Boston to serve as assistant pastor. His future looked very bright, and his mother begged him to accept the call where he could be close to home and loved ones. But young Judson replied: "My work is not here. God is calling me beyond the seas. To stay here would be partial obedience, and I could not be happy with that."

Judah tried to practice partial obedience. She tried to serve both the Lord God and heathen gods (vv. 4,6). But there is no partial obedience. It is either complete obedience or disobedience.

Would this not be a good time for us to evaluate our own lives?

5. Responsible to God. Senator Daniel Webster (1758–1843) was the best-known American orator of his day. While Webster was Secretary of State under President Fillmore, he attended a dinner with twenty gentlemen at the Aston House in New York. Unusually quiet, one man, in an attempt to draw Webster out, asked him what he considered to be the most important thought that ever occupied his mind. Pausing for several minutes, Webster replied: "The most important thought that ever occupied my mind was my individual responsibility to God." With that, he arose and left the room.

This thought ought to be always uppermost in our minds, but like the people of Judah, too often we live and act as though we are not responsible to God. In spite of Jeremiah's warnings and pleadings, Judah closed her eyes and ears and hardened her heart. In 587 B.C. the divine judgment fell upon her when she was carried away into Babylonian captivity, where she remained for seventy years.

TEACHING THE BIBLE

▶ *Main Idea:* God warns the people to trust Him, not their religion and institutions.
▶ *Suggested Teaching Aim:* To identify ways they trust the things of God instead of God Himself

A TEACHING OUTLINE

1. Use an illustration to introduce the Bible study.
2. Use a chart to guide the Bible study.
3. Use volunteer readers to read the Scripture.
4. Use an outside assignment to involve a member in the Bible study.
5. Use list making to give the truth a personal focus.

Introduce the Bible Study
Use "Friends of Jesus?" from "Applying the Bible" to introduce the lesson.

Search for Biblical Truth
Briefly present the seven summary statements in the "Outline and Summary." Point out where Jeremiah delivered his sermon (temple) and why (people trusted temple instead of God). Point out that this likely took place some time after Jehoiakim became king (609 B.C.).

IN ADVANCE, write If and Then on a chalkboard or a large sheet of paper. Call for a volunteer to read verses 3–7. Ask members to identify God's demands ("Amend") in verse 3 and the result if the people obeyed ("cause you to dwell"). Point out that the people believed that God would never allow anything bad to happen to His people and to His holy house.

Call for a volunteer to read verses 5–7. Ask the people to identify God's demands ("If") and the results ("Then"). Write these on the chart. Use "Studying the Bible" to explain the nature of God's demands. Point out the particular social nature of the demands: how they treated others reflected their relationship to God.

Call for a volunteer to read verse 8 and another to read verses 9–11. Point out that the two questions (vv. 9–10 and v. 11) explain what were the "lying words" to which Jeremiah referred in verse 8. Verses 9–10 show that they had convinced themselves that they could practice the worst of sins and still be safe—as long as they continued to go through the motions of worship in the temple.

Ask members to turn to Exodus 20:13–17 and determine which Commandments the people were breaking.

The second question is in verse 11 and it shows that the people's attitude toward the temple was nothing more than how robbers thought about their den. The people thought of the temple as a safe place to stay between crimes.

Call for a volunteer to read verses 12–15. Use "Studying the Bible" to explain the image of Shiloh. IN ADVANCE, enlist a member to prepare a report on Shiloh based on Holman Bible Dictionary. Call for the report at this time. Use "Studying the Bible" to explain the image of Shiloh in Jeremiah.

Briefly summarize the rest of the background passage to conclude the lesson.

Give the Truth a Personal Focus

Ask, What do we trust today that might parallel the way Judah was trusting the temple to keep them safe? (Two examples would be our church membership and baptism.) List these on a chalkboard or a large sheet of paper.

After you have listed all of the members' suggestions, ask what we can expect to happen to us if we trust our religion and its institutions instead of trusting God. Challenge members to place their trust in God alone and to live for Him.

Continuing to Trust

Basic Passage: Habakkuk 2–3
Focal Passages: Habakkuk 2:1–4; 3:17–19

L ike Jeremiah, Habakkuk (huh BAK uhk) was a prophet during the last years of Judah. Also like Jeremiah, he engaged in a dialogue with God in which he expressed some hard questions. Both prophets were perplexed by what was going on around them. They expressed their perplexity to God. In this regard, they were like Job and the writer of Psalm 73. All these people engaged in dialogue with God about the injustices of life. Two facts show that all of these were people of faith: (1) Each expressed his questions to God Himself—a form of prayer. (2) Each continued to trust God even when many questions and problems continued.

▶ ▶ ▶ ▶ ▶ ▶ ▶ ▶ **Study Aim:** *To identify evidences of Habakkuk's trust in the face of existing injustices and expected troubles.*

STUDYING THE BIBLE

Outline and Summary
I. Questions and Answers About Injustice (Hab. 2:1–20)
 1. Patient amid perplexity (2:1)
 2. God's revelation (2:2–3)
 3. Fate of the righteous and the wicked (2:4–5)
 4. Woes on the wicked (2:6–20)
II. Habakkuk's Prayer and Song (Hab. 3:1–19)
 1. Prayer (3:1–2)
 2. Revelation of God's awesome power (3:3–15)
 3. Faith, hope, and joy (3:16–19)

After Habakkuk expressed concern about injustices, he waited patiently for God to answer (2:1). God told Habakkuk that His revelation would surely come, but that it might seem slow by human standards (2:2–3). God's basic answer was that His righteous and faithful people would live, but arrogant and greedy people would perish (2:4–5). A series of woes were pronounced on the latter group for their aggression, exploitation, cruelty, inhumanity, and idolatry (2:6–20). Habakkuk prayed that the Lord would be merciful and renew His works among His people (3:1–2). The prophet described how God's past mighty acts had delivered His people and crushed the wicked (3:3–15). Habakkuk expressed faith, hope, and joy as he awaited a time of troubles and divine deliverance (3:16–19).

I. Questions and Answers About Injustices (Hab. 2:1–20)
 1. Patient amid perplexity (2:1)

1 I will stand upon my watch, and set me upon the tower, and will watch to see what he will say unto me, and what I shall answer when I am reproved.

Habakkuk 2–3 cannot be understood without being tied to chapter 1. Wicked people triumphed over the righteous, and God seemed deaf to the prophet's prayers about such injustices (1:1–4). God answered that He was sending the Chaldeans (kal DEE uhns), another name for the Babylonians (bab uh LOH nih uhns), to execute divine wrath (1:5–11). Habakkuk was even more perplexed by this revelation. He asked how a holy God could use wicked men to overcome others more righteous than they (1:12–17).

Verse 1 of chapter 2 expressed the prophet's determination to wait patiently until God revealed an answer to this dilemma. Habakkuk pictured himself as being like a watchman on the wall of a city. Ancient cities were protected by strong, high walls. A watchman was stationed on the wall to look for an approaching enemy (Ezek. 33:2–6). The prophets were often described as being like watchmen appointed by God to warn against the coming of divine judgment (Jer. 6:17; Ezek. 3:17; 33:7; Hos. 9:8). Habakkuk used the figure to describe the proverbial patience needed by a faithful watchman.

The final line in verse 1 is not easy to understand. The sentence sounds as if Habakkuk expected to be reproved. More likely, the meaning is that he was expecting God's answer to his complaint to prepare him to speak God's word to the people. What is clear is that Habakkuk expected God to provide an answer, and he was willing to wait patiently for God's answer.

2. God's revelation (2:2–3)

2 And the Lord answered me, and said, Write the vision, and make it plain upon tables, that he may run that readeth it.

3 For the vision is yet for an appointed time, but at the end it shall speak, and not lie: though it tarry, wait for it; because it will surely come, it will not tarry.

The word *vision* denotes the supernatural nature of God's revelation. Habakkuk was told to write or inscribe the words on tablets. The tablets could have been of stone, clay, or metal, but clay tablets were more common. When clay tablets hardened, they lasted a long time. Indeed, many ancient inscriptions have been preserved on clay tablets. Thus Habakkuk was to provide a lasting record.

He also was told to make the writing plain or clear. The writing should be clearly read by a runner, either a herald who ran with the message or a person hurrying by where the tablet was displayed.

The need for a lasting record implied that the fulfillment would be in the future. Verse 3 confirms this understanding. The fulfillment would seem to tarry from a human point of view, but it would not tarry forever. It would surely come because it was the word of God. It would come at the time appointed by God. Because God is not bound by human limitations of time, His appointed times often seem unreasonably long to impatient people (see 2 Pet. 3:3–12).

3. Fate of the righteous and the wicked (2:4–5)

4 Behold, his soul which is lifted up is not upright in him: but the just shall live by his faith.

Habakkuk 2:4 is the crux of God's revelation to the prophet about the injustices he described in 1:2–4,12–17. This is also the best-known verse in the Book of Habakkuk.

The first part of verse 4 introduced a revelation that took more shape in verses 5–20. The person whose soul is lifted up in him is an arrogant person. Such a person is the opposite of an upright person. Verse 5 describes arrogant people of insatiable greed. Part of God's revelation is that such people eventually will perish. They may appear to be riding high for a long time, but someday they will reap what they have sown (see Gal. 6:7).

The last part of verse 4 states the positive side of God's revelation. These few words describe the righteous and faithful people of God. God's promise is that they—in contrast to the wicked—shall live. The New Testament gives the full revelation of all that is involved in the words "shall live." Jesus described such life as abundant and eternal (John 3:16; 10:10).

Christians are familiar with the last part of Habakkuk 2:4 because Paul made this a key text for justification by faith (Rom. 1:17; Gal. 3:11). The main idea in the Old Testament word was faithfulness. Faith and faithfulness go together. Sometimes faith is stressed, at other times faithfulness; but in the long run, they go together. Paul emphasized the total reliance on God and not self for salvation, but he made clear that good works and the fruit of the Spirit go with such faith (Eph. 2:8–10; Gal. 5:23–24).

God was contrasting wicked and righteous (just) people in Habakkuk 2:4. Truly righteous people are people of total reliance on God who show their faith in God by their faithfulness to God. Habakkuk's own faith is clear in verses like 2:1 and 3:17–19. These passages also testify to his steadfastness.

4. Woes on the wicked (2:6–20)

A series of woes were pronounced on the wicked because of aggression (vv. 6–8), exploitation (vv. 9–11), cruelty (vv. 12–14), inhumanity (vv. 15–17), and idolatry (vv. 18–20). Because of their terrible sins, judgment was sure. This judgment would fall on the evildoers in Judah and also eventually on the wicked Chaldeans, whom God would first use to punish His people.

Hidden amid these words of judgment are two more positive and memorable verses: "For the earth shall be filled with the knowledge of the glory of the Lord, as the waters cover the sea" (v. 14). "The Lord is in his holy temple: let all the earth keep silence before him" (v. 20).

II. Habakkuk's Prayer and Song (Hab. 3:1–19)

1. Prayer (3:1–2). Habakkuk prayed that the Lord would show mercy to His people by reviving or renewing His work among them.

2. Revelation of God's awesome power (3:3–15). God's awesome power had in the past been exercised for the deliverance of His people and the destruction of the wicked. The Exodus experience of Israel lies behind many of the graphic word pictures of divine power.

3. Faith, hope, and joy (3:16–19). Fear and trembling were Habakkuk's first responses to this dazzling reminder of God's salvation and judgment. The last part of verse 16 shows that the prophet believed the terrible prophecy of the coming of the Babylonians as invaders of Judah (1:5–11). He also believed that at God's appointed time, the Babylonians would themselves be judged (2:5–20) and God's people would be delivered (3:3–15). Habakkuk also knew that, meanwhile, God's people must maintain their faith and faithfulness (2:4). Verses 17–19 show how he responded to these words from God.

> **17 Although the fig tree shall not blossom, neither shall fruit be in the vines; the labour of the olive shall fail, and the fields shall yield no meat; the flock shall be cut off from the fold, and there shall be no herd in the stalls:**
>
> **18 Yet I will rejoice in the Lord, I will joy in the God of my salvation.**
>
> **19 The Lord God is my strength, and he will make my feet like hinds' feet, and he will make me to walk upon mine high places. To the chief singer on my stringed instruments.**

These verses rank among the most amazing expressions of faith in the Bible. At this point in his experience, Habakkuk had much in common with the New Testament teaching to rejoice in times of trouble. This teaching of Jesus (Matt. 5:11–12) was repeated by Paul (Rom. 5:3–4), Peter (1 Pet. 1:6), and James (James 1:2–3). In the same spirit, Habakkuk testified that he would continue to rejoice in the Lord although the worst happened.

Verse 17 describes some of the worst things imaginable in Habakkuk's day and time. People depended on fig trees, grape vines, olive trees, and the other crops for food, oil, and other staples. They also depended on their flocks of sheep and herds of cattle for wool, milk, and meat. Habakkuk knew that when ruthless invaders swept into Judah, all these things probably would be destroyed.

If such a time came, how would the prophet respond? The prophet used the words "rejoice" and "joy" to reinforce the commitment he was making. He testified that if the horrors of verse 17 happened, he would still rejoice in the Lord. How could he rejoice at such a time? He could rejoice because of his confident hope in God's promise that the final outcome would be judgment on sinners and salvation for the faithful righteous.

He also could rejoice because, even as he passed through the worst of times, the Lord God was his strength. Habakkuk even compared himself to the fleet–footed hind or deer. The deer were known not only for their swiftness but also for their surefootedness.

Habakkuk 3 was written like a psalm or song. It was to be set to music. The word "selah" scattered throughout verses 3–15 was a notation to musicians. Likewise, the final line of the book makes clear that the words were to be set to music and sung. The song's note of joyful hope and faith amid trouble has been the testimony of believers down through the centuries.

1. Background. Old Testament scholar Clyde T. Francisco says that the time of Habakkuk's prophecy can be determined with considerable exactness. Assyria is off the scene and Chaldea (Babylon) is coming into power. "The time, therefore, must be after 612 B.C. Judah has not yet been invaded, so it must be before the first invasion[of Judah by Babylon] in 605 B.C. . . . . After the death of [king] Josiah, the people reverted to the sins they were commiting before his reforms." [1]

Judah, it appears had learned nothing from the tragedy of the ten northern tribes. It is the nature of sin to blind sinners to its terrible power and consequences.

2. Why? Habakkuk was a different kind of prophet from those who had preceded him. They spoke for God to the people, but Habakkuk spoke to God for the people. The prophet addressed the inaction of God as the wicked prospered and the people of God languished. He asked God why and waited for God to answer. But his questions were not rebellious ones. [2]

When we get hurt, how often have we asked God why? But that is no sin!

3. Where is God when we need Him? An embittered soldier in Vietnam, who had seen his buddies killed, said, " I'll tell you what is wrong with our world; your God has let us down!"

A university student whose life had been transparent, whose grades were high, and whose future seemed bright was engaged to marry a beautiful girl. On the way to his college commencement he was killed. The family asked bitterly, "Where was God when we needed Him?"

A young couple much in love were anticipating the birth of their first child, but the child was born terribly handicapped. Where is God when we most need Him? Read Habakkuk's brief prophecy and note the questions he asked God. They were also the questions the people were asking. Like us, Habakkuk wondered why God seemed to be hiding when His presence and power were so much in need by Judah. Habakkuk learned that though God delays He is always dependable (3:16ff).

Hope on! Hope in the darkness! God is there too, but he walks among us on quiet feet.

4. Never Alone. The late Dr. Norman Vincent Peale tells about a woman who was trapped in an elevator between floors in a New York City skyscrapper. When the building manager called her on the emergency telephone in the elevator, he asked her if she were alone. "Oh, no," the lady answered calmly. "I am not alone." When finally the elevator was repaired and the lady walked off, the manager looked at her in surprise and said, "But you said you were not alone."

"I was not alone," she replied. "God was with me."

Judah was rebellious, living in opposion to what God had told them to do. They had often been warned to repent and return to God. But their hearts were hard, and they continued in their rebellion. In spite of it all, God was still with them (3:18–19).

In all circumstances—good and bad—God is with the believer, but our sins and lack of faith hinder our fellowship with Him and dull the sense of His presence.

5. Holding on in hard times. Martha Berry founded the Berry School for needy children at Mount Berry, Georgia. A woman of great courage and faith, a 1932 national poll named her one of the twelve outstanding women in America.

Trying to get her fledgling school off the ground, she went to automobile magnate Henry Ford and asked for one million dollars, but he gave her only a dime! She could have felt insulted but, instead, she determined not to let Ford's insensitivity defeat her. Using his dime, Berry bought a bag of peanuts and set her boys to planting them. The next season she planted more peanuts, bagged them and sold them at the nearby crossroads market.

She then wrote Mr. Ford: "Remember that dime? Well, sir, I invested it in peanuts and made enough money to buy a piano for my music students. How's that for dividends?"

Ford was so impressed with her courage and optimism that he invited her to Detroit where he presented her with a gift of one million dollars!" [3]

Habakkuk asked a good many questions about the conditions that prevailed in Judah. But his faith in God's love and power never waned. Habakkuk closes his book with a great exclamation of faith and joy (3:17–19).

As we face difficulties that try our faith, let us follow Habakkuk's example. Faith shines a light in the darkness and we move on (Rom. 8:28).

TEACHING THE BIBLE

▶ *Main Idea:* God calls His people to trust in the face of existing injustices and expected troubles.
▶ *Suggested Teaching Aim:* To identify elements that will help adults trust God in the face of injustice and trouble.

A TEACHING OUTLINE

1. Use an illustration to introduce the lesson.
2. Use a chart, brief lectures, and group discussion to search for biblical truth.
3. Use a paraphrase and/or hymn writing to interpret Scripture.
4. Use brainstorming to apply the Scripture to members' lives.

Introduce the Bible Study
Use "Where is God when we need Him?" to introduce the lesson.

Search for Biblical Truth
Briefly set the context of these verses by overviewing the summary in "Studying the Bible."

On a chalkboard or a large sheet of paper, write:

Stand ("stand upon my watch")
Set ("me upon the tower")
Watch to see ("what he will say")
("what I will answer when reproved")

Call for a volunteer to read Habakkuk 2:1 and ask members to complete the above chart by adding the material in parentheses and explaining Habakkuk's questioning and faith.

Ask members to look at 2:2–3. Ask: Why do you think God wanted Habakkuk to write the message on tablets? (Let them respond. Consider this: it was going to be a while before the message was fulfilled and God wanted to be sure the message survived.)

DISCUSS: Why do you think God delays in executing His judgment on the wicked?

Read aloud 2:4. Ask members to look at Romans 1:7 and Galatians 3:11. Point out that the main idea of the Old Testament word for *faith* was "faithfulness" Because God's people were faithful to Him, they would live. The wicked would be destroyed. Use "Studying the Bible" to explain the New Testament use of this significant passage.

Briefly summarize the material in "Studying the Bible" for 2:6–3:16 so members will be able to understand the climax to the book.

DISCUSS: How can we develop the faith to be faithful to God in times of crisis? What does our faithfulness say about our faith in God? Call for a volunteer to read 3:17–18. Call for this verse to be read in as many different translations as you have. Use the comments in "Studying the Bible" to point out the marvelous expression of faith voiced by Habakkuk. Distribute paper and pencils and ask members to paraphrase these verses. Encourage them to use modern events in their writing.

As an alternate activity, ask members either individually or as a group to paraphrase these words so they can be sung to an existing hymn tune (such as "All the Way My Savior Leads Me" or some other tune in the same meter.) Sing the hymn as a conclusion to the lesson.

Give the Truth a Personal Focus

Ask, What made Habakkuk so confident in his trust in God? Write members' comments on a chalkboard or a large sheet of paper.

Next ask them to evaluate their own lives to see which of these qualities they need to add so that they can develop a similar faith and faithfulness. Point out that we have the benefit of God's divine record of faithfulness to His people in the Bible and 2,500 years of history proving He does care for His people. In addition, we have the Holy Spirit to guide us and support us in our tasks.

If members wrote a hymn, read or sing it in closing. Close with a prayer encouraging members to trust God in the face of injustice and trouble.

---

1 Clyde T. Francisco; *Introducing the Old Testament*, rev. ed. (Nashville: Broadman Press; 1977), 1977.

2 Ibid.

3 Robert Hastings in *Proclaim* (January/February/March 1993): p. 28. From Margaret T. Applegarth, "Twelve Baskets Full," *Harper's* 1957, 124–25.